Kyle C.

Living A Life Of

Luxury

With Little Money

Disclaimer

The content of this book represents the personal views, ideas, perceptions, interpretations, and understanding of the author. It is intended solely for informational, educational, and reference purposes. The material presented in this book is not offered as professional advice of any kind, including but not limited to legal, financial, psychological, medical, or technical advice.

The views and opinions expressed are entirely those of the author and do not necessarily reflect the positions, beliefs, or policies of any organisation, institution, employer, government body, or individual with which the author may be or may have been affiliated. Any names, events, or scenarios mentioned are referenced in a generalised context for illustrative purposes.

Readers are strongly encouraged to engage with the material critically and independently. While the content draws from the author's personal experiences, interpretations, and observations of the world, it is not intended to be authoritative or definitive. Interpretations may vary, and readers are urged to verify facts, consult relevant sources where appropriate, and draw their own conclusions.

This book also seeks to provoke thought, challenge assumptions, and raise questions about systems, beliefs, and perspectives that shape modern life. It is not written to enforce agreement but to stimulate reflection and encourage deeper inquiry. The author makes no guarantees regarding the accuracy, completeness, or applicability of the content in all contexts and disclaims any liability for actions taken based on the material presented.

Use of the information in this book is at the reader’s own discretion and responsibility.

All the images in this book have been digitally processed using AI, primarily to remove identifying details such as names or specific locations associated with the objects depicted, ensuring privacy or anonymity.

Introduction

We work hard every day to earn money to cover our basic expenses like food, shelter, bills, transportation and others to keep our lives moving. Some of us barely make it through the month. Rent eats a third of the pay. Groceries go up but wages stay the same. Even small things, like a flat tyre or a higher electricity bill, throw the balance off. It becomes a cycle where survival feels like success.

When we make more than we need, we will use the money for some luxuries in life, like that brand new Mercedes, a designer handbag, or the new gaming rig. It is not just about the object. It is the moment we feel in control. A way to say, finally, this part of my life is mine. We tell ourselves we deserve it. Sometimes we do. Sometimes we just want to feel like we are not falling behind.

Purchasing expensive things has never been made easier with a variety of options out there. You can walk into a store with nothing in your wallet and still walk out with a thousand-dollar item. Credit cards, buy now pay later, personal loans and many more to help one to make huge, expensive purchases where one could enjoy the expensive things and pay them back later via monthly instalments. You do not need to think about the total. Just the monthly breakdown. It tricks the mind. The trap is not in the price, it is in the illusion of affordability. By the time you add it all up, you are already buried.

Peer pressure from families and friends contributed to the culture of showing off and enjoying expensive things to prove that you are successful in life. It is silent but constant. You feel it in the jokes, the comparisons, the way someone looks at your shoes or asks when you are upgrading your phone. You see people younger than you flaunting what you cannot afford. You wonder if you are behind, even when you are holding things together better than they are. Social media is flooded with people flashing their new designer bags and merchandise. No one posts the interest payments. No one shows the stress behind the smile. It is all surface, and it feeds the loop.

It is not wrong to enjoy life if you can afford it. After all, you have busted your ass in life to get where you are today. You have worked when sick, skipped meals, stayed late, and done things you hated just to pay the bills. If you want to enjoy what you earned, you should. You should not feel guilty for reaching for more. All of us wish for a nice, comfortable life with some bragging rights. Not to boast, but to remind ourselves that we are not stuck anymore. That we made it through.

Different individuals enjoy their lives differently. Some create a collection of expensive designer products, not just for fashion but because it makes them feel like they have arrived. Others put their money into upgrades that no one else sees: a better mattress, a full fridge, a new lock on the door. The point is never the thing. It is what it means: to feel secure, to feel seen, to feel free from the fear of falling back.

Living a life of luxury and indulgence remains a cherished dream for many. We imagine owning a grand house, driving a sleek car, surrounding ourselves with designer brands and finer things. This vision often fuels our determination and pushes us to work harder day after day. It feels like the ultimate goal, a symbol of success and achievement that motivates countless individuals. However, reaching that level of affluence is far from simple. For most people, it remains elusive. Recent reports on personal debt reveal a troubling trend: many accumulate mounting credit card bills just to buy expensive goods or embark on lavish holidays. Then they showcase these purchases on social media, chasing the approval of likes and boosting their ego. Such a lifestyle demands significant financial resources, and very few can sustain it without serious strain. Unless you are already a multi-millionaire or billionaire, maintaining that kind of extravagance is nearly impossible over the long term.

Interestingly, those who have genuinely achieved great wealth often do not live in such a flashy or ostentatious manner. They do not chase after every new luxury trend or attempt to impress others with extravagant displays. To them, comfort takes precedence over showiness. Their idea of living well means having enough space to feel at ease, owning tools and possessions that simplify daily life, and driving vehicles that save time rather than merely turn heads. While all these comforts require money, the focus is on quality, utility and efficiency rather than excess. Their approach is measured and practical, grounded in the understanding that true luxury lies in convenience and ease, not in ostentation.

But what if there were ways to enjoy a lavish lifestyle without needing to earn millions? What if you could experience comfort, style, and some of the finer things without plunging into debt or spending beyond your means? This book aims to explore precisely that possibility. I will share practical methods and insightful tips on how to bring a taste of luxury into your life without breaking your bank account. The secret lies not in how much you earn but in your mindset, in prioritising spending on what truly matters and what you can afford responsibly.

As the old saying goes, borrowing to invest in assets can be wise, while taking on debt for liabilities is foolish. And accumulating too much debt is simply reckless. Learning to distinguish between these choices is essential for anyone who wants to live well without sacrificing financial stability. This book will guide you on that path, showing how you can enjoy life's pleasures sensibly, with balance and foresight.

Rent, Not Buy

Rent first, not buy into a property before you are ready. It is a simple piece of advice that many overlook in the rush to claim ownership. Buying a property is not just about having a place to live or an asset to your name. It is a commitment layered with financial responsibility, long-term planning, and an understanding of your own stability.

If you have just started working and are earning a stable salary, you should avoid falling into the same trap that many in the older generation did. One of the most common mistakes was rushing into buying property, especially a high-rise apartment, under the belief that it is a smart financial move. In the past, owning a property meant owning the land it was built on. That land held intrinsic value and it could appreciate independently of the structure. These days, things are different. When you purchase an apartment in a high-rise, you are not buying a piece of land. Instead, you are purchasing a portion of a building that you must share with hundreds of others. The land belongs to everyone in the building collectively, which removes the individual value that used to come with property ownership.

If you consider all the aspects, buying an apartment might not be a wise financial decision at all. You will end up committing to a mortgage that eats up a large chunk of your income every month. On paper, it may seem manageable, but once the cost of living, property maintenance, and unexpected fees pile on, it can quickly become overwhelming. Worse still, you will be sharing the building with people you have no control over. These strangers will come and go, and the environment can change dramatically within a few years. You could begin in a decent community, but there is no guarantee it will remain that way.

I made this mistake myself. After landing my first job, I was eager to show that I was responsible and ready for adulthood. I bought a modest two-bedroom apartment, thinking it was a stable investment and a milestone worth reaching. For a while, it worked out. The building was relatively clean, the neighbours were polite, and everything seemed in order. But then, everything started to shift. The building management changed hands. The new company did not maintain the facilities properly, and cleanliness began to decline. Routine maintenance was delayed or ignored. The lift broke down more frequently, security was no longer consistent, and complaints were often met with silence or excuses.

As conditions worsened, the atmosphere inside the building changed. More and more units were being rented out, and many new tenants treated the place with little respect. Shady characters started appearing, and it became clear that some units were being leased for short-term stays with no proper screening. The building no longer felt safe, and what once had the feeling of a home started to feel more like a rundown hotel. Property values dropped. The surrounding neighbourhood followed suit. Businesses closed, public cleanliness declined, and the area slowly lost its appeal.

The people who were financially able to move out began leaving one by one. They cut their losses and found better places to live. I was not as lucky. I still had to make monthly mortgage payments and did not have the resources to relocate. Selling would have meant accepting a significant loss, and renting the unit out would have brought its own risks. I found myself stuck, trapped by a decision I had made in good faith when I was younger and less experienced.

Things started to improve after I took a new job at another company, which required me to move to a different area. This new company offered some options when it came to accommodation. They gave me the choice to either stay in the housing they provided or receive a fixed monthly allowance for accommodation expenses. After weighing the options, I decided to take the allowance instead of the company's housing. The reason was simple: the company-provided accommodation was located quite far from the city centre, which made commuting to work inconvenient and time-consuming. I did not want to spend hours each day travelling back and forth, so I preferred the flexibility of renting my own place closer to work, even if it meant paying a little extra out of my own pocket.

The housing allowance was limited and did not cover the full cost of most of the nicer apartments near my office. Despite this, I decided to take the risk and rent a luxury apartment in a convenient location with access to all the amenities I wanted. The rent was about thirty percent more than the allowance I received each month, which meant I had to allocate part of my salary to cover the difference. It was a financial stretch, but I felt it was worth every penny for the quality of life I gained.

I no longer had to endure long, crowded commutes. I could avoid the stress of packing into buses and metro trains during rush hour. Getting to work became a quick and easy journey. On weekends, grocery shopping was a simple task. Several supermarkets and shops were within walking distance, making it easy to pick up fresh ingredients and essentials without hassle. The neighbourhood was filled with plenty of cafés and eateries, giving me options for days when I did not feel like cooking.

Cooking itself was something I enjoyed. I treated it like an art form and a way to unwind after a stressful day at work. Having a well-equipped kitchen and easy access to fresh produce made the experience even more satisfying. It became a creative outlet and a means to relax, rather than just a chore.

The apartment complex offered a range of excellent facilities. The gym was fully equipped, clean, and spacious, allowing me to maintain my fitness routine. There were jacuzzis where I could relax and soothe my muscles after exercise. The infinity pool overlooked the city skyline and was a favourite place to unwind. For residents who needed to work from home or hold small meetings, the business lounges were available and well maintained.

Because of the shorter commute and the location of my apartment, I saved a significant amount of money that would have otherwise gone to transport costs. I did not own a car, so I avoided expenses related to petrol, insurance, maintenance, and parking fees. My monthly expenses were straightforward and manageable. Apart from food and utility bills, my largest expense was the rent. Thankfully, the rent included security fees and building maintenance costs, so I did not have to worry about extra charges or managing upkeep myself.

Living in this apartment gave me a comfortable lifestyle with a touch of luxury, all while keeping my spending reasonable. I enjoyed modern conveniences and peace of mind in a safe environment close to work and the city's amenities.

My parents have always insisted that I buy a property of my own. Their argument goes that owning a place gives you complete freedom to do what you want with it. That sounds good in theory, but not when it comes to apartments. Their thinking is stuck in a different time. I have decided to buy a property somewhere on the outskirts, a place to retire, instead of a small apartment where I would constantly worry about all the expenses that come with ownership. These include property taxes, on top of the maintenance fees and other charges I have mentioned before. As for freedom, owning a property can actually tie you down if you live in it. Since I was working somewhere else, I rented out my apartment to help cover the mortgage payments. The rental income covered about sixty percent of the mortgage in the current market. Some people might be quick to shout, "See? Owning a property is not a bad idea because you are collecting rent!"

That is true to an extent. Owning property can be profitable if it generates income. But living in your own property often feels like a liability because you are constantly paying the mortgage and other costs. There are also risks and stress that come with renting out your place to strangers. If you are lucky and have a good tenant who always pays on time, that is ideal. But if you end up with a tenant from hell, it becomes a nightmare. You deal with delayed or missing rental payments, unpaid water and electricity bills, and possibly legal fees if you have to evict them.

Property no longer holds the guaranteed promise of being a reliable investment instrument. In many regions, the market is saturated with an excess of houses, and more continue to be constructed year after year. While property values might rise over time in some cases, they are equally capable of falling. Recent events in California illustrate this reality starkly. The devastating fires that swept through vast areas have caused property prices in those affected locations to plunge dramatically. What once were highly sought-after neighbourhoods, coveted for their views and amenities, have transformed into the places where owners are desperate to sell. The fear of recurrent disasters has gripped potential buyers, leaving many unwilling to take the risk of investing in a home vulnerable to such calamities. Consequently, prices have spiralled downwards as the demand evaporates. This situation reveals that property investment, which many once considered a safe bet, now carries significant uncertainties. Investors must be vigilant and consider factors beyond mere location and aesthetics, such as environmental risks and broader market conditions, before committing their hard-earned money.

Owning a property is a major responsibility that demands proper planning and extra cash to cover any unexpected costs. If I could start over, I would probably choose to rent a nice place in a convenient location that saves me time and money. Then I would use the extra funds to invest in stocks, ETFs or improve myself by learning new skills that could turn into a side hustle.

Comfort and convenience are the main criteria when selecting a property. Rent first before consider buying

Another important factor to consider when deciding to rent is whether you need a car. For many people, owning a car feels like a necessity. It offers convenience and freedom to travel whenever and wherever they want without relying on public transportation schedules. However, owning a car comes with a long list of expenses: monthly loan payments, petrol costs, insurance, maintenance, parking fees, and unexpected repairs. These costs can add up quickly and eat into your monthly budget.

In my case, living near everything I need has made owning a car unnecessary. My accommodation is close to work, grocery stores, cafes, and other essential places. For daily errands and commuting, public transportation works perfectly. The buses and metro are reliable and affordable, so I do not have to worry about traffic or parking issues. This setup has saved me a significant amount of money and stress.

On the rare occasions when I need to travel somewhere that public transport does not reach or is inconvenient, I simply use ride-hailing services like Grab or Uber. These services are widely available and provide a flexible alternative to owning a car. They allow me to get where I need to go without the long-term commitment and costs associated with car ownership. I can request a ride only when necessary and avoid paying for fuel, parking, or maintenance.

By choosing this approach, I have managed to keep my expenses manageable while still maintaining freedom of movement. This is an advantage many people overlook when considering whether to rent or buy property. The convenience of living in a well-connected location means I can get around easily without the burden of a car. For those who live in less accessible areas, owning a vehicle might be unavoidable. But for me, not having a car has been a practical decision that fits well with my lifestyle and financial goals.

If you happen to have some extra cash, you can elevate the experience by opting for a ride in a luxury car. Instead of settling for the usual economy options, selecting a premium vehicle through ride-hailing apps adds a touch of comfort and style to your journey. Whether it's a sleek sedan or a spacious SUV, the ride becomes smoother, quieter, and far more enjoyable. This choice is perfect for special occasions, important meetings, or simply when you want to treat yourself without the hassle of owning a luxury car. It lets you enjoy the benefits of luxury travel on demand, without the long-term financial commitment or maintenance costs that come with car ownership.

Live Minimally, But Aesthetically Pleasing

Living in a minimalist yet aesthetically pleasing space can have a profound impact on your psychological well-being. Feng shui principles emphasise how the arrangement of furniture, the flow of natural light, and the overall comfort and cleanliness of a room contribute to creating an environment that feels balanced and calm. Natural light entering a space lifts your mood and sharpens focus, helping to reduce stress and fatigue. Comfort, whether found in the texture of your furnishings or the layout of your room, invites relaxation and makes daily life more enjoyable. Cleanliness clears visual clutter, which in turn clears mental clutter, making it easier to concentrate and feel at ease.

If your income allows you to secure a place of your own in a good location, it is wise to plan carefully before rushing into extravagant renovations or purchasing expensive furniture. Instead of immediately aiming to turn your home into something overly ornate or luxurious, such as a palace-like setting, it pays to take a step back and consider your actual needs and lifestyle. Today's generative AI tools provide excellent opportunities to visualise your design ideas in advance. These tools can help you explore different colour schemes, furniture placements, and decorative styles digitally, saving time and money compared to trial and error with physical renovations.

Before the advent of AI, I created concept art with Photoshop and reached out to interior designers who offered complimentary 3D renderings in hopes of securing renovation projects. My first home renovation reflected my inexperience. I installed grand chandeliers and completely reworked the tiles throughout the house. I added many cabinets and storage spaces, convinced I would make full use of them. The renovation cost far more than I had anticipated.

In reality, many features went unused. I never turned on the chandeliers, preferring the simple LED lights and spotlights for daily illumination. Most of the storage cabinets remained nearly empty, except for my bookshelf in the home office, which was full due to my love of reading. My parents appreciated the extra storage, coming from a generation that grew up during times of scarcity. Their experience of wartime shortages instilled a habit of keeping supplies like plastic bags and bottles for future use.

My approach is different. I avoid collecting items without real value. Sorting and recycling plastic bottles and cans feels like a chore I prefer to avoid. I choose to live a minimalist lifestyle, focusing on simplicity and utility. I keep only possessions that provide genuine satisfaction or a sense of achievement when displayed. This mindset helps me avoid clutter and creates a living environment where everything serves a purpose.

So, what should you be collecting? Start with gold and precious metals. These have long been regarded as reliable stores of value. They retain worth over time and often act as a safeguard against inflation or economic uncertainty. Unlike many other assets, gold does not depend on the success of a company or government policies. Its intrinsic value makes it a solid choice for anyone interested in preserving wealth.

Another worthy collection is proper artwork, such as sculptures and paintings that require real skill and craftsmanship. Avoid the so-called modern art that lacks substance or technique; much of it tends to be more about hype than genuine artistic expression. Instead, focus on acquiring or creating art that reflects your own vision and creativity. When you make your own art, you are expressing your individual perspective rather than purchasing someone else's interpretation. This personal involvement adds deeper meaning and connection to what you keep in your home.

Rare items like old coins also make valuable additions. Collecting these pieces is not about showing off to friends or visitors, although it might impress them. More importantly, you are preserving a tangible fragment of human history. Each coin tells a story about a time, place, and culture long gone. Such collections can educate and inspire, reminding us of the passage of time and the evolution of societies.

If purchasing high-end collectibles feels out of reach, there are simpler ways to begin curating a personal collection that brings joy and character to your living space. Starting with porcelain or pottery pieces for your shelves offers an accessible and elegant introduction to collecting. Choose items that speak to your taste, whether delicate vases with intricate patterns or rustic pots with unique textures. Alongside these, bring life and tranquillity to your home by arranging some indoor plants in a small, zen-inspired garden. Use oddly shaped stones scattered thoughtfully among the greenery to add natural contrast and intrigue. This arrangement, whether placed in your living room or a quiet corner, creates a calming refuge within your everyday environment.

Another way to enrich your space is by enhancing the lighting. Position spotlights to highlight your own handcrafted pieces displayed on pedestals or shelves. The focused illumination not only accentuates their beauty but also casts soft shadows that add depth and warmth to the room. Every glance at these objects will serve as a reminder of your efforts and achievements, an affirmation of the hard work that led to their acquisition or creation. This subtle yet powerful boost to your mood can transform an ordinary day, instilling a sense of positivity and pride that carries you through challenges with renewed energy. By curating your surroundings thoughtfully, you build not just a collection, but a personal sanctuary that reflects your journey and aspirations.

This is an illustration of a simple DIY project at home.

Concept art for a corner in your house, if you have the passion and time

Having beautiful, well-chosen items around you can brighten your mood and create an environment that feels both welcoming and luxurious. Incorporating gold pieces and tasteful decorations can also improve the *Feng Shui* of your home. *Feng Shui* is an ancient Chinese practice that focuses on arranging your living space to promote harmony, balance, and positive energy flow. The idea is that the way you place furniture, colours, and objects influences the energy, known as "Chi," that moves through your space, affecting your health, happiness, and prosperity.

A home filled with clutter or random, neglected items can feel chaotic and heavy, almost like a slum. Such an environment can weigh down your spirit and create stress. On the other hand, a space designed thoughtfully with clean lines, meaningful objects, and elements that bring you joy encourages a peaceful and uplifting atmosphere. This kind of environment not only looks pleasing but also nurtures your mental wellbeing.

There is also an important connection between your surroundings and your behaviour. Just as bad company can increase the likelihood of poor choices, living in a disorderly or negative environment may impact your mindset negatively. Conversely, surrounding yourself with positive influences, whether through the people you meet or the environment you create, can help improve your character and outlook. Being around intelligent, motivated individuals tends to sharpen your own thinking and drive.

Because your surroundings have such a powerful effect, it is vital to plan your living space carefully. Taking the time to arrange your home to support your mood and personal growth will help you become the best version of yourself. Your environment should inspire and energise you, not drain or distract you.

A smooth flow of energy through your living space helps everything in life progress with ease. When your environment is balanced and harmonious, daily tasks feel less like a struggle and more like a natural rhythm. On the other hand, a cluttered or negative space can weigh you down, filling your life with obstacles and unnecessary complications. It creates mental and emotional blockages that make even simple things harder than they need to be.

Having gold and precious ornaments that carry intrinsic value can draw positive energy and wealth towards you. These items not only add beauty to your surroundings but also act as symbols of prosperity and success. Their presence reminds you of abundance and helps create an atmosphere where opportunities can flourish. When your home reflects value and care, it sends a message to the world and to yourself that you are ready to receive good fortune.

These ideas serve only as a starting point. Ultimately, discovering your own style and preferences is what truly matters. The design you choose should uplift your mood, create a sense of comfort, and provide genuine pleasure whenever your eyes rest upon it. There is no single formula or rule to follow; it is a personal journey shaped by your tastes and the atmosphere you want to cultivate.

You might consider experimenting with different styles as a creative side project, testing out various arrangements and themes to see which resonates with you the most and endures over time. Observing what feels natural and what you find yourself drawn to repeatedly will guide you towards a design that truly fits your life.

If you enjoy change or have the time and energy to do so, refreshing the look from time to time can inject a burst of energy and positivity into your daily routine. Small updates or seasonal tweaks can make your space feel alive and dynamic, offering a fresh perspective every day.

Above all, the design should serve your needs and desires, not create stress or feel like a burden. It must work in harmony with your lifestyle and personality, enhancing your environment rather than complicating it. When your surroundings support and reflect who you are, every moment spent there becomes more enjoyable and meaningful.

Quality over Brand Names

Designer brands are mainly for bragging rights to show others that you have made it. Humans often judge others through the first impression, sometimes in just seconds. If you dress well, talk in a good manner, and drive an expensive car, others will immediately think, “Wow, you are really successful,” even when you could just rent a suit for the occasion, brush up your talking skills the night before, and borrow the car from your successful cousin. Those surface details create an image that many people accept without question. No one will ask about the truth behind it until they get to know you personally.

The phrase, “Never judge a book by its cover,” or even Chinese phrases like “The person looks down on another with the dog’s eyes,” teach us the same lesson across different cultures. That is how we are built. Our brains take in visual cues and sensory information to make quick conclusions. If a person looks shady or out of place, our minds would definitely scream, “This guy is a freaking thief for sure.” I’m not saying that it is a bad thing. These instincts exist to help us stay out of trouble. They make us more alert to people whose behaviours match the negative image our minds create. Over time, those behaviours often prove the initial impression right.

Back to the designer brands. I like designer stuff. I won’t lie. Well, who wouldn’t like nice, beautiful things, right? Most people are obsessed with having big brand names on their clothes, wallets, handbags, shoes, or whatever else they carry around, because they think the brand alone will boost their social status. The logos speak louder than words, shouting, “Look at me, I am bloody rich!” That is how years of marketing, social media, and celebrity culture have trained people to think. A label stitched on the corner suddenly makes a plain item feel exclusive. That association between big names and luxury is drilled into our heads until it becomes automatic.

When you trace the origins of brand names, their purpose was never about showing off or making a statement of wealth. Initially, they served a simple but essential function: to identify the product as belonging to a particular company or designer. The label was a mark of origin, a way to say, "This comes from our workshop," or "This is authentic, crafted by us." It was a straightforward declaration of ownership and authenticity, a practical means of distinguishing one maker's goods from another's.

Over time, these names grew beyond their original role and evolved into symbols of quality and reliability. Consumers began to associate certain brands with trustworthiness, knowing that products bearing those labels had met a certain standard. The brand became a guarantee of sorts, an assurance that the item was well made, carefully produced, and worthy of attention. It was a relationship built on identity and confidence rather than extravagance or status.

However, as time passed, this concept gradually shifted. What was once about recognition and trust began to twist into something else entirely. Brand names morphed into badges of social standing, symbols used to flaunt wealth and success rather than simply convey authenticity or quality. The original meaning became clouded, replaced by an obsession with image and status. The emphasis moved away from the craftsmanship or the story behind the product, focusing instead on the prestige attached to the brand names.

The business trip to Shanghai had been a mixture of long meetings and cultural discovery. One particular experience stood out sharply. Our local business partner took us to a market famous for selling imitation products. These were no ordinary fakes. They were graded by quality. The highest grade was astonishing. The items looked exactly like the authentic goods. The partner explained that these top-tier imitations actually came from the very factories producing the genuine articles. It was a world where the line between real and fake blurred almost entirely.

I decided to buy a pair of unbranded shoes. They had no flashy logos or brand name stitched on the side. Meanwhile, my colleague went straight for a Louis Vuitton wallet, the same brand he already used daily. He said it made sense to have a spare just in case. Not stopping there, he also picked up a leather wallet bearing a local Chinese brand. At first, it felt odd to trust these unknown names alongside the prestige of Louis Vuitton.

Back home, the reality surprised us both. My pair of unbranded shoes endured everyday wear and tear better than my Nike shoes. They matched the toughness and comfort I expected only from my Timberland boots. My colleague's Chinese branded leather wallet outlasted both the genuine Louis Vuitton one and the imitation wallet from the market. It was a striking lesson. Quality mattered far more than the brand's reputation.

From that moment on, our focus shifted completely. We stopped chasing brand names for status or image. Instead, we concentrated on the real value of what we were buying. Quality became the deciding factor. That trip changed how we viewed products and the importance of brand labels. What counted was durability, craftsmanship, and practical use, not the name stitched into the leather or printed on the shoe tongue. The experience taught us to look beyond the brand and appreciate what really matters.

Now it is less about what you are wearing and more about what name is printed on it. The louder the name, the more attention it pulls. But honestly, truly rich people do not care about brand names like that. They already have money. They have nothing to prove to anyone. That is the whole point. When you have real wealth, you do not need to shout about it. You just wear what you like, whether it has a logo or not. What is there to prove when everyone knows you are rich?

Designer stuff nowadays are marketing schemes that brainwash you into thinking that you can buy success just by wearing them. That somehow slipping on a branded jacket or carrying a luxury bag will turn you into someone powerful, admired, and accomplished. It is a trick, really. A carefully built illusion that tells you, "If you wear this, you will be seen as important." These products are not just clothes or accessories anymore. They are tools to boost your ego. They feed that craving to feel like you matter more than the next person. They are products made to "package" yourself into someone you are not. Someone richer, someone more refined, someone who seems like they belong at the top. It is like putting on a costume and hoping others will believe the character you are playing.

If you like to enjoy life with a bit of luxury but do not want to waste your money, and you are hooked on designer stuff, then you ought to start by changing your mindset. There is nothing wrong with liking designer brands. It is perfectly fine to enjoy them, but you do not need to over-indulge or get swept away by the hype. I do buy some designer products myself. The difference is, whenever I make a purchase, I pay attention to the quality instead of going in blindly just because of a flashy brand name. I use the brand as a guide, not a reason. A name tells me about the company's history, their craftsmanship, and what they are known for.

Recently I bought a Mont Blanc pen and wallet. Sure, there are brands out there that people would say are "better," like Louis Vuitton, Burberry, and others. But I chose Mont Blanc because I liked the quality of the leather. It felt solid, smooth, and durable, not something that would wear down in a year or two. That was ten years ago, and my wallet still looks pristine. No cracks, no loose stitching, no fading. That, to me, is a proper investment. Every time I use it, I still enjoy the feel of the leather. It reminds me that I made a smart choice. On the same day I bought it, my friend got an LV wallet at the same mall. He liked the name and wanted the logo. It did not even last him two years.

With the tariff and trade war between the United States and China, many manufacturers that produce goods for luxury brands came out and exposed the real costs behind those products. It caused quite a stir in the online community. People were shocked, and rightfully so. Items that were being sold for thousands turned out to cost only a fraction to make. It broke the illusion for many and raised questions about what exactly people were paying for. Was it the craftsmanship, or just the brand name slapped on the surface?

But in the end, it comes back to you. You should be a wise consumer. Always remember that the brands are there to serve you, not the other way round. Do not turn yourself into a slave for a name. Do not let it define your value. Use the brand as a tool, not a trophy. Let it act as a seal of quality, something that tells you, "Yes, this is made well," not something you use just to prove yourself to others.

I still shop around and buy from small, unknown brands. I value quality above all else. I am simply too lazy to deal with things that break easily or wear out too quickly. I want to buy something once and be done with it for years. After quality, the next thing I look at is design. A well-designed item, no matter how simple, can lift your mood and create a positive vibe around you. At home, I have a huge Ikea shelf that takes up an entire wall, where I display my collection of porcelain and all kinds of unique pieces I have found at flea markets and little trinket shops. Every time guests come over, they pause in front of the shelf and start gasping. I get the usual comments like, "Wow, these must be expensive," or "These are probably worth a fortune," when in truth, many of those pieces cost me under ten dollars. Some were just a few pennies, and a few were even free, handed to me by the shop owners who just wanted to clear space.

What's interesting is, some of the items turned out to be worth far more than I paid, simply because they were old enough to be considered antiques. One time, I was working on a small DIY project and needed something to fill a glass container. I had found this beautiful container with 24k gold-plated trims, and I wanted to make it look like it belonged in some royal collection. I thought of using gold beads to fill it, but real ones would cost a fortune and fake ones just looked cheap and ruined the aesthetic I was going for. Then I came across a bag of old coins at a flea market. The seller was asking for a hundred dollars. I looked through the bag and saw that most of the coins were from the late 1900s, not particularly rare or valuable. I bargained a little and managed to get the whole bag for twenty dollars, which felt like a reasonable deal. The seller was clearly trying to clear everything out and seemed glad to let it go.

When I got home, the first thing I did was clean all the coins. I wanted to get rid of whatever dirt, germs, or whatever else might have been left behind from the hands of who-knows-how-many people who touched them before me. As I scrubbed through them, I noticed something surprising. Two coins were from the Victorian era, with Queen Victoria's face engraved on them. A few others carried the face of her son, King Edward VII. Those immediately stood out and fit perfectly inside the new container. Once arranged, the entire piece looked like a display straight out of a museum. The coins blended beautifully with the glass and gold trim. It became more than just a decorative item. It carried stories from the past, sealed in a simple container that now sits on my shelf as a quiet tribute to history.

My trip to Japan brought in even more loot for my collection. While my friends were busy roaming around luxury brand stores, chasing limited edition items and queuing up outside boutiques, I headed straight for the largest second-hand store in Tokyo. That place was massive, filled with every imaginable item from watches to tea sets. I wandered through the aisles and eventually stumbled upon a boxed set of 24k gold-plated sake glasses. They were tucked away on a low shelf, almost hidden behind a row of dusty cups. The set looked barely used, with the original packaging still intact and lined with soft velvet. I picked them up without hesitation.

24k gold-plated sake glasses

They had a variety of designs, from the national emblem to detailed carvings of dragons, mountains, and plants. Each piece was unique, displaying careful craftsmanship with fine details that caught the eye. What made it even better was the price; each glass cost around four dollars, dirt cheap for something so well made. After giving them a thorough wipe, the gold colour gleamed brightly under the lights, far more vibrant and genuine-looking than any fake gold or brass material I had seen before. As soon as I placed them on my shelf and turned on the spotlights, the whole collection suddenly looked expensive and impressive. It transformed the space instantly.

A good piece of clothing depends on the materials used in making them. Do they make your skin rash? Are they comfortable? Do the clothes make you look better? These questions are essential because the quality and type of fabric directly impact how the clothing feels against your skin and how well it fits your body. If the material irritates your skin or causes discomfort, no matter how stylish the garment looks, it will never feel right or help your confidence. Simply slapping your body with designer clothing and accessories will not make you look fabulous. Instead, it will only make you look ridiculous and like a "show-off" jerk who keeps flaunting your wealth. This kind of behaviour usually stems from ego rather than true style or personal expression.

The rich back then wore silk, not hemp with a brand.

Living rich means you put on quality clothing that shows the best version of yourself. A clean, simple, and tidy look will make everyone feel comfortable, confident, and trusting you more. When your outfit is well put together without being over the top, you naturally attract better connections with those around you. These are the little luxuries in life that money cannot buy. You also do not have to spend a lot of money on a good piece of clothing. That does not mean you should only buy from Walmart or cheap stores. Some designer stores offer good quality clothing that fits you well and stands the test of time.

Every piece of clothing acts as an accessory to complement the real you. Brand names won't help you with that. It is the combination of comfort, style, colour, design, and how well everything matches that will project the image of you. Billionaires such as the late Steve Jobs, Mark Zuckerberg, and Jeff Bezos often wore simple, possibly expensive clothing due to the materials used, worn daily. Their goal was to be the image that they envisioned along with comfort in daily wear. They prioritised themselves, not to please others or feed their ego by showing off how rich they really are.

Be Your Own Chef

Dining in a fancy restaurant? Well, it is a treat once in a while. But dining there every day? You are not getting the value worth from it. Most of what you pay goes to the salary of the workers and the rental of the restaurant space. If you have extra cash to spend and prefer to enjoy dining for the service and ambience, then by all means, go ahead, since you are contributing to the economy, which is a good thing. But if you can't afford to dine at fancy restaurants daily, there are still ways to enjoy a similar dining experience in the comfort of your own home. I am an avid cook who prefers to shop for my own groceries, selecting the ingredients I like. I have never liked food that is overly complex, except for curry, where some chefs try out multi-layered textures and tastes. I prefer to be able to taste each ingredient clearly. Also, it is healthier to prefer food at home since you know exactly what goes into the meal. I have even had the unpleasant experience of finding extra roaches in my meal at an expensive place.

The best food in the world is about simplicity while still being fulfilling, though this varies from person to person. For me, a simple meal like good bread is perfect, not the soft, mass-produced Wonder Bread, but proper bread baked in an oven with a crusty outside and a soft, fluffy inside. Paired with cheese and butter, it feels like a match made in heaven. I could eat that for every meal without growing tired of it.

Nothing beats a freshly baked bread with butter and cheese

Another favourite is a simple sunny-side-up egg seasoned with soy sauce, freshly ground pepper, and shredded dried *kombu,* eaten alongside a bowl of steamed rice. The combination is humble yet satisfying, comforting in its straightforwardness.

Sometimes I prefer something heartier, like a stew. Slow-cooked beef, seasoned and combined with carrots, potatoes, and turnips, becomes tender after hours of gentle heat. Occasionally, I make a basic pottage with a variety of vegetables, including Chinese cabbages, which add a subtle sweetness to the broth. Stews are the easiest dishes to prepare. You chop the ingredients, add seasoning, place them in a crock pot or Dutch oven, and let it cook slowly while you attend to other tasks. When I am not making stew, I turn to soups. Chicken and beef soups are staples in my kitchen, but sometimes I experiment by simmering chicken stock with Chinese cabbages and scallops, blending delicate flavours into a soothing broth.

Cooking calms me. It sharpens my mind and sparks creativity. It is a space where I can test ideas freely and see the results without fear of judgement, well, except maybe from family members if I am cooking for them. The process of trial and error, experimenting with recipes and improvising, always brings me a great deal of joy.

Simple sausages and mash

Meat and potatoes stew

Beyond the art of cooking, I take considerable care in ensuring the dining table always looks impeccably arranged. Each element has its place, from the polished silverware to the carefully selected array of glasses. There is a distinct glass for wine, another for whiskey shots, and a separate one for ordinary drinks. Even the water pitcher is actually a large whiskey decanter, adding an unexpected touch of elegance. The entire setup creates an atmosphere that feels both expensive and refined, lifting the mood around the table even when the meal itself is less than perfect.

I have not spent a fortune acquiring these items. Most were purchased at modest prices but look far more luxurious than their cost would suggest. Many came from big sales or clearance events, the kind of opportunities that reward patience and attention. There is a satisfaction in finding bargains that do not sacrifice quality. When something is reasonably priced, well made, and improves everyday life for years to come, it becomes an investment worth making. The careful curation of tableware is more than decoration; it reflects pride, hospitality, and the desire to create memorable experiences in a setting that feels special without breaking the bank.

Arranging the table with carefully selected pieces brings a subtle elegance that turns an ordinary meal into something memorable. It goes beyond mere decoration; the very act of setting the table alters the atmosphere, inviting everyone to slow down and savour the moment. The placement of each plate, glass, and utensil signals that this time is special, encouraging mindfulness and a deeper appreciation of the food and company. Such a setting transforms eating into a ritual, making each bite much more pleasurable.

Pairing this thoughtful environment with cooking your favourite dishes elevates the entire experience. It becomes not just about nourishment but also about creativity and personal growth. As you experiment with recipes, adjusting flavours and trying new techniques, you engage with your food in a way that is both fun and fulfilling. The kitchen turns into a space of discovery where mistakes are lessons and successes bring joy. Through this process, you improve your culinary skills while enjoying the satisfaction of crafting meals that delight both the palate and the soul.

A well-chosen decoration on the dining table says more about you than you might realise. It acts as a subtle reflection of your personality, your tastes, and the atmosphere you wish to create for those who gather around it. This space, often overlooked in comparison to the living room, holds a special significance. It is where families come together to share meals, stories, and moments of connection. Friends often find themselves seated here, caught in conversations that stretch long into the evening.

The dining table serves not only as a functional spot for nourishment but also as a stage where your character is quietly displayed. The choice of centrepieces, the style of placemats, the type of crockery provide the details that speak of the care and attention you invest in your home and the people you invite into it. When guests notice the thoughtfully arranged candles or a vase filled with fresh flowers, they sense something deeper. It is not just decoration but a message of welcome and warmth.

In many ways, this setting becomes a canvas for personal expression. It allows you to share a part of yourself without words, conveying your appreciation for beauty, order, or perhaps a love for simplicity. The dining table transforms into more than just a place to eat. It becomes a place to show who you are to those you hold dear, making each gathering a little more special and memorable.

My simple dining table setup

Some concept arts, if you are feeling fancy.

Take Care of Your Body

You have probably heard the saying "Health is wealth" countless times in your life, whether through television, radio, advertisements, social media, or even during casual chats with friends. It is a phrase so familiar that it often fades into the background, yet the truth it carries remains undeniable. Without a healthy body, you cannot enjoy anything life has to offer. No amount of wealth, luxury, or success can compensate for the physical suffering that comes with poor health. In reality, the money you spend years trying to earn will eventually be redirected toward endless visits to doctors, ongoing medication, and rising insurance premiums that come with a deteriorating condition.

Despite how simple and obvious this truth seems, very few people actually treat it as a priority. Healthy eating becomes the first thing to be sacrificed. Rather than investing time and care into preparing well-balanced meals, you reach for instant food options that are cheap, heavily processed, and quick to cook. These become staples not out of choice but from a lifestyle shaped by constant rushing and convenience. Instead of making space for rest and recovery, you take on more work. You stay longer at the office, volunteer for overtime, and squeeze in side jobs just to collect a bit more money, while quietly pushing your body beyond what it can reasonably handle.

Examples of this behaviour and its consequences are everywhere. There was news from China involving food delivery riders, many of whom worked themselves to death. In an industry built on speed and quantity, they rushed through traffic day and night, trying to complete as many orders as possible to earn commissions and stay ahead of the crushing competition. With minimal rest and overwhelming pressure, their bodies eventually gave in. In some heartbreaking cases, they were found slumped over on their motorbikes, having taken a short break that became permanent. They had died from pure exhaustion, their lives quietly extinguished in between deliveries.

Personally, I am guilty of this as well. In the early years of my career, I was heavily influenced by those around me, particularly the older generation, who constantly repeated phrases like "work hard, play hard" or "if you work hard enough, you will get somewhere." These beliefs were not just words. They were the unspoken rules of the workplace. Management consistently rewarded those who clocked the longest hours, often ignoring actual results in favour of those who stayed the latest, skipped breaks, or made themselves highly visible through empty flattery. I had a job that paid decently, and I pushed myself to the limit. There were periods where I went without sleep for three days straight just to complete a project on time. The company incentivised this behaviour by offering performance bonuses to staff who managed to deliver results, on top of the standard annual bonuses and salary increments.

Financially, I was doing well. I was raking in good money, but I paid for it with my health. My weight doubled. My body ballooned in size. Simple tasks like climbing a short flight of stairs left me breathless. I relied on caffeine daily just to stay functional, but it completely threw off my sleep cycle. The constant stimulation wrecked my internal clock. Headaches became normal. My blood pressure shot up, making it difficult to breathe properly. These symptoms were not occasional. They followed me every day, clinging to every hour like a shadow. My body was falling apart. At one point, I even passed out in a hotel room after returning from a client visit. I had pushed too hard, and my body had nothing left to give.

Sure, I was able to afford a comfortable stay at a five-star hotel during that business trip. I even upgraded my flight to business class at my own expense, simply because I could. I thought I might as well enjoy a little luxury after everything I had pushed through. On paper, everything looked ideal. I had the money. I had the means. I had the status. But with a body in that condition, none of it meant anything. The food served in the executive lounge tasted bland. The wine that others savoured tasted bitter on my tongue. The pounding in my head refused to ease, even as I lay on the soft, high-thread-count sheets of the hotel bed. I could not relax. I could not enjoy a single moment of what I had paid for. Was it worth it? Not at all.

When I finally tried to step back and negotiate some time off, I kept my request clear and measured. I asked for between three to six months of paid leave to recover, even offered to work from home during the period so I could gradually regain strength without compromising entirely on responsibilities. I requested to cut down on business travel completely. I sent my proposal through the proper channels. I waited for a response. Management did not even acknowledge the request. Instead, what I received next was a formal letter offering a significant increase in remuneration. My salary was raised by fifty percent. I was promised company stocks, offered at no cost, to be granted when the company eventually went public. The projected valuation was in the seven-figure range.

In exchange, they asked for one thing. I would need to maintain the same level of performance and delivery for the next ten years. The offer was structured like a golden reward, but buried in the fine print was a set of conditions that resembled a tightly bound contract. It was not just an incentive. It was a bond. One that required everything I had left.

The amount stated in the contract was undeniably tempting. On paper, it looked like a once-in-a-lifetime opportunity, something that could secure a future beyond what most people could ever hope for. But beneath the surface, it was a bad deal. The fine print spelled out conditions that completely changed the nature of the offer. The company stocks that had been presented as a generous reward would only be granted after ten full years of continuous service. There was no guarantee that the estimated seven-figure value would still hold by the time those shares were actually issued. The market could shift. The company could restructure. The numbers were projections, not promises.

Even the salary increase that seemed so immediate at first glance was broken into a drawn-out schedule. Instead of receiving the full fifty percent raise from the following month, the adjustment would be spread across a three-year period, divided into annual increments. The most alarming clause, however, was buried further down. If the management determined at any point during those ten years that my performance was no longer meeting expectations, they reserved the right to revoke the entire agreement. All benefits could be cancelled without prior warning. On top of that, I could be held liable for breach of contract and made to repay the financial advantages already received. It was a trap wrapped in numbers. The risks were placed squarely on me, while the company held all the control.

Maintaining the performance was never the real problem. Maintaining my health was. I once made a joke to my former colleagues about the contract offer. If I were to accept it, I would probably end up working from a hospital bed. The extra income would be funnelled into paying for a private suite in a hospital, while the rest would go towards medication and treatment. That was not the life I had imagined when I thought about financial success. That was not the future I had worked so hard for.

Not long after, I made the decision to resign from that position. I accepted a new job that offered thirty percent less than what I had previously earned. On the surface, it looked like a downgrade, but in reality, it was the best decision I could have made. The salary was more than sufficient to cover all my expenses, and I still had a comfortable amount left to save or spend as I pleased. More importantly, the new job allowed me to rest. Overtime was extremely rare, as the company operated on a subscription-based revenue model rather than project-based earnings. There was no pressure to chase deadlines or travel across countries to meet clients. All meetings were conducted through video conferences.

Within just six months, the difference was remarkable. My health improved significantly. I no longer needed medication to manage my blood pressure, as I had begun spending my free time on meditation and proper rest. My weight returned to a healthy range. I had more energy. I was finally able to enjoy the life I had spent years building towards. With the money I had saved from my previous role, I invested wisely, creating multiple income streams that could continue supporting my lifestyle without the need to compromise my health again.

To be able to enjoy and experience things in a healthy body is a luxury itself.

Be More Sophisticated

Take up a hobby like reading or painting. Be more sophisticated. That's what people often say when they want to sound cultured. But what does sophistication really mean? It's not about appearing fancy to others. True sophistication comes from within. It's about enriching your inner life and approaching each day with intention.

Fill yourself with knowledge. Wealth is not just about having lots of money. Knowledge is equally important with having money. I've come to realise this truth more deeply as I've grown older. Money comes and goes, but what you know stays with you forever.

Let me tell you something about books. They're magical in a way that's hard to describe until you experience it yourself. I started reading seriously about five years ago. Before that, I was always "too busy" or "too tired" after work. Now I can't imagine my life without my daily reading ritual. It's like having conversations with the greatest minds throughout history, right in your living room.

I prefer physical books over digital ones. There's something special about holding a real book in your hands, feeling the weight of it, smelling that distinct paper scent that digital just can't replicate. My bookshelves have become a physical representation of my mental journey. Every time I look at them, I see not just books but markers of different phases in my life, different questions I was trying to answer.

Knowledge acquisition isn't just about books though. It's about approaching life with curiosity. When I travel, I don't just see the standard tourist spots. I talk to locals, try to understand their perspectives. When I meet someone with a different background, I ask questions and listen more than I speak. Every person you meet knows something you don't.

Have a morning tea or coffee routine. Read physical books. Journal. These daily habits create a sense of richness and control over your time. The morning coffee ritual has become sacred to me. I wake up thirty minutes earlier than I need to just so I can enjoy this time without rushing.

I grind the beans myself. The sound and smell wake up my senses before the caffeine does. I use a French press because I enjoy the process, the waiting, the pressing down slowly. Then I sit by my window, cup in hand, and just exist for a while. No phone, no news, no emails. Just me and my thoughts and the sunrise. It costs almost nothing but feels incredibly luxurious. That's thirty minutes of my day that belong completely to me.

Journaling has changed my life in ways I never expected. I used to think it was silly. Write down my thoughts? Why? I'm having them, I know what they are. But there's something transformative about putting pen to paper. Thoughts that seem crystal clear in your head often reveal themselves as muddled or incomplete when you try to write them down. The act of writing forces clarity.

I keep it simple. Just a notebook and pen beside my bed. Sometimes I write for pages, other times just a few lines. There are no rules. Some days I write about big life questions, other days I just note what I'm grateful for or what I hope to accomplish. Looking back at old journals is fascinating. You see patterns you couldn't notice in real time. You witness your own growth.
Painting is another hobby that has brought richness to my life, though I'm certainly no professional. I never painted as a child and felt intimidated at first. What if I was terrible at it?

Then I realised that I was missing the point entirely. The value isn't in creating masterpieces but in the process itself.

When you paint, you have to really see the world around you. Not just glance at it, but truly observe. The way light falls across a face, how colors blend and contrast, the infinite varieties of green in a single tree. It makes you notice details in everyday life that you would otherwise miss completely. Plus, there's something deeply satisfying about creating something tangible, even if it's just for yourself.

These habits aren't expensive or flashy. They won't impress strangers or look glamorous on social media. But they create a foundation of daily satisfaction that money simply cannot buy.

I've known wealthy people who rush through their days, constantly checking emails, always busy but never present. And I've known people of modest means who approach each day with intentionality and awareness, who seem to experience more life in a week than others do in a month. That second group always seems happier to me.

I believe in creating pockets of richness in ordinary days. A simple meal prepared with care and eaten without distraction. A conversation where you're fully present, not half-thinking about something else. A walk where you notice the changing seasons. These moments cost nothing but feel incredibly abundant.

Physical spaces matter too. You don't need a mansion to create an environment that feels good to return to. Clear out the clutter. Have fewer things but make them things you truly enjoy. I have a reading corner with my favourite chair, a good lamp, and a small table just big enough for a cup of tea. It's nothing special objectively, but it's become a space that feels right to me. Creating your own spaces rather than following trends makes your home feel truly yours.

Libraries are incredible resources that many people overlook. I visit mine weekly. Not just for books, but for the community events, the lectures, the film screenings. All free, all enriching. The wealth of resources available through public institutions is staggering if you take the time to explore them.

Learning new skills keeps your mind flexible and gives you confidence that extends to other areas of your life. I decided to learn to bake bread from scratch last year. The first few loaves were disasters. Dense, undercooked in some spots, burnt in others. But each failure taught me something, and now I can reliably produce a loaf that tastes better than anything I could buy. The process taught me patience and observation, and there's something deeply satisfying about creating something so fundamental with your own hands.

Conversations are another form of wealth often overlooked. Not the surface-level small talk that fills most social gatherings, but real exchanges of ideas and perspectives. I've found that asking better questions leads to better conversations. Instead of "What do you do?" try "What are you excited about lately?" Watch how the energy changes.

Deep friendships take time and nurturing but are worth every moment invested. Having people in your life who truly know you, who you can be completely yourself with, creates a sense of security that no amount of money in the bank can provide. These relationships require maintenance though. Regular check-ins, remembering what matters to them, being there during difficult times, celebrating their successes without envy.

Nature provides endless sophistication for those who pay attention. I try to spend time outdoors every day, even if it's just ten minutes. The changing light throughout the seasons, the cycle of growth and rest, the incredible variety of living things all around us, even in cities. It's a constant reminder of how much bigger the world is than my daily concerns. There's nothing more humbling or more reassuring.

Sleep is underrated in our culture. We brag about how little we get, as if it's a badge of honor. But good sleep is foundational to experiencing life fully. I protect my sleep schedule religiously now. The bedroom is for sleeping only, no screens allowed. I read physical books before bed instead. My thinking is clearer, my emotions more stable, my energy more consistent when I prioritise rest.

Cooking from scratch connects you to food in a way that takeout never can. Understanding ingredients, learning techniques, experiencing the transformation of raw elements into something nourishing and delicious, this is profound stuff that we've outsourced almost completely in modern life. It doesn't have to be complicated. Some of the best meals consist of just a few ingredients prepared simply but with attention.

Financial wisdom is part of sophisticated living too. Not the obsessive pursuit of wealth, but understanding money as a tool rather than a goal. Knowing the difference between spending that creates lasting value and spending that just fills a temporary void. Being intentional about where your resources go.

I've found that tracking expenses, not just paying bills but really looking at where the money goes each month, was eye-opening. So much was going to things that provided no real satisfaction. Redirecting those funds toward experiences or items that genuinely enhanced my life made me feel instantly wealthier without earning a penny more.

Time is the ultimate non-renewable resource. We all get the same amount each day, regardless of our bank balance. How we use those hours determines the richness of our lives more than anything else. I now evaluate potential commitments by asking "Is this worthy of my time?" rather than just looking at financial compensation or social obligation.

Many people rush through life, always focused on the next achievement, the next acquisition, the next goal. They reach the end having checked all the boxes but feeling somehow cheated, as if they missed something essential along the way. That something is the present moment, the only time we ever truly have.

Mindfulness doesn't require hours of meditation or spiritual belief. It's simply the practice of paying attention to what's happening right now. The taste of your food. The feeling of sunshine on your skin. The expression on a loved one's face as they talk. These moments, fully experienced, create a tapestry of richness that requires no financial investment.

Social media and constant connectivity have eroded our ability to be present. I've set boundaries around technology use. No phones during meals. No checking email first thing in the morning or last thing at night. Designated periods where I'm completely offline. The world doesn't end, and my experience of life becomes immediately more vivid.

Creating something, anything, brings a satisfaction that passive consumption never can. Writing, cooking, gardening, building, painting, music, crafts. The medium doesn't matter. What matters is the shift from consumer to creator, from spectator to participant. Even amateur efforts bring joy and meaning that purchased experiences rarely match.

Travel with intention rather than just ticking off destinations. Before visiting somewhere new, I learn about the history, read literature from that place, perhaps try cooking some traditional dishes. The experience becomes richer, more textured. And it doesn't have to be exotic locations. Sometimes exploring your own region with fresh eyes can be just as rewarding.

Cultivate gratitude not as a forced exercise but as a genuine recognition of abundance already present. Notice what's going well, what beauty exists in your daily life, what problems you don't have. This isn't about ignoring real challenges but about maintaining perspective.

In the end, sophisticated living isn't about impressing others or accumulating status symbols. It's about crafting a life rich in meaning, knowledge, beauty, and connection. It's about being intentional with your time and attention rather than letting circumstances or cultural defaults dictate your experience. It's about recognising that true wealth exists in how fully you live each day, not in what you own or how you appear to others.

Take up a hobby like reading or painting. Be more sophisticated. Fill yourself with knowledge. Have a morning tea or coffee routine. Read physical books. Journal. These aren't just pleasant suggestions. They're pathways to a fundamentally different experience of being alive. An experience where every day contains moments of richness, where time feels abundant rather than scarce, where life is something to be savored rather than survived.

The most sophisticated people I know aren't necessarily the wealthiest or most educated. They're the ones who have mastered the art of being present for their own lives, who approach each day with curiosity and intention, who create pockets of beauty and meaning in ordinary circumstances. That kind of sophistication is available to anyone willing to cultivate it, regardless of their financial situation. And once you experience it, no amount of money seems worth trading it for.

Once you become skilled at your hobby, the next step is to consider turning it into a source of income. Begin small by treating it as a side hustle, something that runs alongside your current commitments. As your product gains interest and demand grows, and once you have built a group of loyal customers who appreciate what you offer, you can then focus on expanding your efforts. It is important not to rush the process but to allow your work to develop organically. Building a steady client base takes time, and only when you see consistent support should you invest more energy and resources. This gradual approach helps ensure that your hobby grows into a reliable and sustainable venture.

Some real-world examples show how this approach works. Take Xiaomi. It began by listening to its community, offering quality products at affordable prices. It did not try to compete with the biggest brands immediately. Instead, Xiaomi grew by refining products, building trust, and rewarding loyal customers with better services. This steady growth made Xiaomi a global technology player.

OnePlus started as a small brand founded by a few individuals aiming to make high-quality smartphones without steep prices. Its reach was limited at first, but it focused on tech enthusiasts. OnePlus built a loyal fan base through word of mouth and careful launches. They improved with each release. What began as a side project became a respected smartphone brand.

Create a Signature Scent or Style

Finding a unique and affordable perfume or settling on a consistent style of dress can be a simple yet powerful way to create a signature presence. It is about crafting an identity that feels distinct and refined without the need to spend excessively. Whether it is a scent that lingers in the air after you leave a room or a carefully curated wardrobe that reflects your personality, having a signature style can set you apart in subtle, meaningful ways.

Imagine walking into a five-star hotel or an exclusive boutique catering to the wealthy. The instant you enter, your senses are greeted by a soothing and luxurious scent. That fragrance is no accident. High-end establishments invest in distinct perfumes to create a memorable atmosphere, one that leaves guests feeling special and comforted. The scent itself can transform a space, making it feel lavish and inviting. It is not uncommon for these hotels to use custom blends or premium fragrances designed to evoke a sense of calm and opulence.

Interestingly, in places like Hong Kong, there are shops that sell imitations of these luxury hotel fragrances. They allow people to bring a slice of that luxury home. However, these perfumes come with a price. The cost is not just in the initial purchase but also in maintaining a steady supply to keep the scent alive over time. Continually restocking the fragrance can add up quickly, sometimes becoming a sizeable expense. This approach, while effective, may not be the most practical or economical choice for everyone.

On the other hand, crafting your own perfume offers a different kind of satisfaction. Making a perfume is not just a creative endeavour; it is a deeply personal one. For those who enjoy do-it-yourself projects, it provides an opportunity to experiment and develop a scent that perfectly suits their preferences. The process can be fun and rewarding, especially for someone new to perfumery who is willing to explore and learn.

The internet is filled with countless tutorials that guide beginners through every step of perfume-making. From understanding the basic components to mixing and balancing different notes, these resources provide a comprehensive introduction to the art. Starting with simple recipes using essential oils or fragrance oils, even those without prior experience can create appealing blends. This DIY approach offers control over the scent profile. You can adjust the balance of floral, woody, citrus, or spicy notes until you find a combination that feels truly yours.

Moreover, making your own perfume allows for endless customisation. If you find that a particular scent is too strong, too subtle, or missing a certain character, you can tweak the formula. Unlike commercial perfumes that come fixed in a bottle, your creation can evolve with you. You might begin with a fresh, light citrus base for summer and later add deeper, warmer elements for cooler months. This flexibility ensures your signature scent stays fresh and relevant to your mood and style.

Besides the satisfaction of creation, DIY perfume can also be more budget-friendly. While initial supplies like essential oils, carrier oils, alcohol, and bottles might seem like an investment, these materials can last a long time. A few drops of essential oil go a long way, and you only need to combine small quantities to make batches. Over time, this can prove cheaper than buying multiple bottles of luxury perfumes or constantly refilling expensive hotel-scented sprays.

Developing a signature style of dress goes hand in hand with finding a personal scent. Style is another way to communicate who you are without words. It need not be about chasing trends or wearing the most expensive brands. Instead, it is about understanding what makes you feel confident and comfortable. A consistent style could mean choosing a colour palette that complements your skin tone, adopting a particular silhouette that flatters your body shape, or selecting fabrics and textures that reflect your personality.

The key to a signature style is consistency. Wearing a similar style regularly creates a visual identity that others begin to associate with you. It signals self-awareness and intentionality, qualities that often come across as refined. For example, a person might always opt for well-tailored blazers paired with classic jeans and simple accessories. Over time, this becomes their trademark look, effortlessly elegant and recognisable.

This approach also helps in managing expenses. Instead of buying random pieces to chase fleeting trends, investing in timeless basics can be more economical and sustainable. Pieces like a well-cut white shirt, quality denim, neutral-toned trousers, or a classic coat are versatile and last across seasons. By mixing and matching these staples, you can create multiple outfits without overspending.

Adding signature elements to your wardrobe can further elevate your style. This might be a favourite pair of shoes, a particular style of bag, or accessories like scarves or hats that add personality. These details, when chosen carefully, enhance the overall look and contribute to a coherent style that feels unique.

Pairing your signature style with a distinct scent can amplify your presence. When someone meets you, the combination of how you dress and the fragrance you wear leaves a lasting impression. The scent adds an invisible layer to your style, subtly influencing how people perceive you. It can convey warmth, elegance, freshness, or mystery depending on the notes you choose.

Returning to the idea of scents in luxury settings, the reason these perfumes feel so impactful is because of the attention to detail. Luxury hotels and boutiques often use complex fragrance blends composed of multiple layers or notes. These layers unfold gradually, with a top note that is immediately noticeable, a heart note that develops after some time, and a base note that lingers long after. Understanding these elements can help when creating your own perfume or choosing one to make your signature.

The top note is what you smell first. It is usually light, fresh, and evaporates quickly. Common top notes include citrus scents like lemon, bergamot, or orange, as well as herbal elements like mint or lavender. The heart note appears once the top note fades. This is the core of the perfume and lasts longer. Floral scents like rose, jasmine, or ylang-ylang often make up the heart. The base note provides depth and longevity. These heavier scents, such as sandalwood, vanilla, or musk, are what remain on the skin for hours.

When selecting or creating a perfume, balancing these layers ensures the fragrance is well-rounded and dynamic. A perfume that only has a strong top note might fade quickly and feel one-dimensional, whereas one with a strong base note but no refreshing top could seem heavy or overwhelming. Experimenting with these elements is part of the joy in creating a unique scent.

Making perfume at home can also be a mindful ritual. The process of blending oils and crafting a scent can be calming and creative. It encourages you to slow down and pay attention to subtle differences in aroma. Over time, you may develop a more nuanced appreciation for fragrances and the way they interact with your skin chemistry.

To start making your own perfume, you will need a few basic ingredients and tools. Essential oils or fragrance oils provide the scent. Carrier oils such as jojoba or sweet almond oil dilute the essential oils and make them safe to apply to the skin. Alcohol, usually high-proof ethyl alcohol, can be used as a base to help the fragrance spread and evaporate evenly. You will also need small glass bottles for storing the finished perfume, droppers or pipettes for measuring, and mixing containers.

The process typically begins by selecting your essential oils based on the scent profile you want. For a fresh and uplifting perfume, you might choose lemon, grapefruit, and lavender. For something warm and sensual, sandalwood, vanilla, and patchouli could work well. Start by blending small amounts and adjusting until you achieve the balance you like.

After mixing your oils with the carrier and alcohol, the perfume should be left to mature for a few days or weeks. This resting period allows the scents to meld together, resulting in a smoother and more harmonious fragrance. Once ready, transfer your creation into a spray bottle for easy application.

Besides perfumes, you can extend your signature scent concept to your living environment. Using scented candles, diffusers, or room sprays that reflect your personal fragrance can make your home feel inviting and luxurious. The same principles apply: select scents that resonate with you and create the atmosphere you desire.

Ultimately, finding a signature scent or style is about self-expression. It gives you a way to present yourself that feels authentic and considered. It does not require extravagant spending or chasing fleeting trends. With a little creativity, patience, and experimentation, you can develop a refined and memorable presence that leaves a lasting impression wherever you go.

Invest in Personal Development

Read, write, learn a new language, practise public speaking, or study philosophy. Growth does not cost much but it adds deep value to life in ways you might not immediately realise. Among all forms of personal development, one I would definitely recommend is public speaking or presentation skills. Pay attention to how successful presenters captivate their audiences. Notice the way they engage with the crowd, how they use their voice, gestures and eye contact to make the message clear and persuasive. They do not just relay information; they sell ideas, convince people to see things from their perspective and keep listeners hooked from start to finish. Having strong business presentation skills or the ability to speak confidently in public opens up tremendous opportunities in any career. You will get chances to present in front of top management teams at major companies or directly to business owners who are rich, powerful and influential. These moments allow you to engage with key decision-makers, create a strong impression and potentially change the course of your career.

I had several opportunities to give presentations to senior leaders due to the nature of my job. At first, it was far from easy. I was nervous and sometimes stammered during my talks. I would lose my train of thought and the stress showed on my face. Then everything changed during a difficult time when I was stuck in a job I hated. It was not the actual work I disliked but the people above me who were completely incompetent. They made a mess of many things, including my responsibilities. They forced me to take on tasks that were not part of my role, then retroactively made those tasks official parts of my job without offering any additional pay or recognition. The constant pressure and unfair treatment pushed me close to the edge. I seriously considered resigning. The final blow came when they made me present project progress updates to top management, something the project manager should have done. At that time, I was just a low-level designer with no authority. I had no intention of putting up with their shenanigans any longer. I did not care if they decided to fire me. I was one step away from handing in my resignation letter.

During that particular presentation, I did not feel nervous at all. I stopped worrying about how my managers or the audience would judge my appearance or whether I was saying the right things. My mind focused solely on the solutions I had to present. I wanted to finish the presentation so I could hand in my resignation immediately afterwards. To my surprise, the presentation went very well. The client clearly understood what I had presented and we had a detailed discussion after the session. The sense of relief was so strong that I completely forgot about quitting. When the next presentation came around, I maintained the same mindset. Over time, after several presentations, I became the main presenter for all the projects. The experience transformed my confidence and skills. Through ongoing interactions with clients, I built close and genuine relationships with some of them. They invited me out to lunch at fancy restaurants whenever I visited their offices. I was even given rides in their expensive cars. During Christmas, some clients gave me generous gifts to thank me for completing their projects successfully.

However, all these experiences and gifts were not as valuable as the connections I had built over time. Those relationships, formed through honest work and countless project discussions, turned out to be worth far more than any material thing. When I finally tendered my resignation, I did not even need to search for a new job. One of the clients, who had been consistently impressed by the way I handled his projects, immediately reached out to offer me a role. He gave me a package that was more than 30% higher than what I was earning at the time, and threw in a few perks on top of that. And he was not the only one. A few other clients also got in touch the moment they heard I was leaving. They appreciated the work I had done, and they did not want to lose that connection. Some of them offered me roles in their companies too. I ended up choosing the one that gave me the best mix of freedom, learning opportunities, and pay. I joined that company and stayed there for a solid ten years. A full decade of work, growth, and trust. Eventually, when I felt the time was right, I walked away to build my own company from scratch. But I never lost touch with those clients. We stayed in contact, shared updates, and kept the professional relationship alive. When I launched my company, those same clients who once sat across from me in meeting rooms became my first batch of customers. They supported me straight out of the gate, and because of them, my company got the early momentum it needed.

Living in luxury does not mean surrounding yourself with overpriced things or throwing money at branded items just to feel important. Real luxury is about comfort, peace, and a sense of fulfilment that satisfies both your mind and your body. It is the kind of life where you wake up without stress, where you enjoy the work you do, and where the people around you add value to your life rather than drain it. My interactions with clients played a big role in shaping that kind of life for me. Every meeting, every discussion, and every project brought a different kind of richness to my mental state. Those experiences, full of stimulating conversations and unexpected insights, gave me a deeper appreciation of the work I was doing. I was not just clocking in and out. I was building something meaningful with people who respected what I brought to the table. After that, money came without much struggle. Opportunities showed up more often, and getting paid well became a side effect rather than the main focus.

When you develop personal skills, you are not just improving yourself in isolation. You are opening doors. You are giving yourself the chance to put your name out there and show the world what you are capable of. These skills become your platform, allowing you to connect with people who share the same mindset and values. As the saying goes, "Great minds think alike." When you start building those connections, it is like laying down highways across your life. Each one leads somewhere different. Some bring opportunities you never saw coming. Others bring in knowledge, partnerships, money, even fame. It is not just about learning to speak better, present better, or lead better. It is about creating a network of paths that push your life forward in every direction. The more skills you build, the more highways you create, and the further you can go. There are no limits once the right people know what you can do. You become the kind of person others want to work with, follow, and trust. And from there, your possibilities are endless.

Some people might argue that in order to promote yourself, you need to spend a lot of money. That might hold true if you are running a new company or launching a fresh product that requires instant visibility. In those cases, pouring money into marketing is often the fastest and most effective method to get noticed, but it is also far from cheap. However, if you are not aiming for mass exposure or trying to break into a competitive market overnight, there are other ways. You can take the slower but more meaningful route by building genuine relationships and forming connections through real conversations and trust. That was exactly what I did. Honestly, the cost was close to nothing. Maybe a bit here and there on mobile data or an occasional SMS just to say hello and keep in touch. Now and then, I paid for lunch or coffee when we caught up, but those small gestures were hardly a burden. The value I got in return from those connections was far greater than any marketing budget could buy.

Once that foundation is in place, you will find yourself ready for the next stage, which is not just about networking anymore. It is about cultivating a rich, engaging social life filled with meaningful relationships that keep on giving.

Cultivate a Rich Social Life

We have a limited lifespan in this world. No matter how much wealth we accumulate, none of it can follow us beyond our final breath. The legacy we leave behind is not measured by our bank accounts but by the impact we have on the lives of others and the memories we create with those we love. Relationships are the real treasure and nurturing them can bring a deep sense of fulfilment that no material possession ever could. Money can buy convenience, luxury and comfort but it cannot purchase sincerity, loyalty or genuine companionship. In moments of joy, it is those we care for that we long to share our happiness with. In times of sorrow, it is their support that gives us strength. Investing in strong, meaningful connections transforms ordinary moments into cherished memories. It enriches the human experience far beyond what any amount of wealth can offer.

Consider this: would you rather sit alone in a mansion with riches beyond imagination or laugh around a humble dinner table surrounded by true friends who care about you, not your status? The answer is clear to those who understand the irreplaceable value of real relationships. Friends who uplift us, who walk with us through storms and sunshine, give us a richness of life that is irrefutable.

There are those who seek companionship through wealth. They attract people with lavish parties, expensive gifts and grand gestures. But such relationships often hinge on the presence of money. When wealth vanishes, so too does the attention and the so-called friendships. These bonds built on material offerings lack the foundation of trust, care and mutual respect. They are hollow and fleeting.

Sadly, this is not just a hypothetical scenario. Across the world, countless individuals have experienced the painful realisation that their social circles were only as strong as their financial standing. People once surrounded by admirers and sycophants find themselves abandoned when misfortune strikes. This phenomenon may seem like a tale from a film but in truth, it mirrors the harsh realities of human behaviour.

You may have witnessed it in your own workplace. Colleagues who fawn over powerful managers only to shun them the moment they lose their position. These acts are not born from genuine respect or affection but from self-interest. When power or wealth is no longer present, the incentive to maintain the pretence disappears, revealing the superficial nature of these interactions.

That is why cultivating a rich social life should not be about quantity but quality. A handful of sincere, supportive and trustworthy friends can have a far greater impact on your life than a crowd of people who offer nothing beyond small talk and shallow praise. It is important to be intentional with friendships. Seek depth over breadth. Build bonds that are anchored in shared values, mutual respect and authenticity.

One powerful way to deepen these bonds is through shared experiences. Hosting potluck dinners, for instance, is not just about food. It is about creating space for connection, storytelling and laughter. Each person brings something to the table, not just a dish but a piece of themselves. It fosters a sense of community and belonging, reminding us that we are not alone in this journey.

Going for walks together, engaging in deep conversations or even enjoying a quiet moment side by side can strengthen the ties that bind us. These simple acts, though often overlooked, have the potential to create lasting impressions. They require nothing more than time and willingness but yield returns far greater than any monetary investment.

The essence of a rich social life lies in consistency and presence. Showing up for each other not just in celebrations but also during struggles is what defines true companionship. It is not always grand gestures that matter but the quiet, everyday moments of care and consideration. Checking in on a friend, remembering a birthday,

listening without judgement. These actions build the foundation of lasting relationships.

Additionally, embracing vulnerability is key. Opening up about your fears, failures and hopes invites others to do the same. It creates a safe space where honesty flourishes and pretence falls away. In such spaces, trust is nurtured and bonds are solidified. Vulnerability is not a weakness but a bridge that connects hearts.

Moreover, cultivating a rich social life requires a certain level of emotional intelligence. Empathy, patience and active listening are essential traits. Understanding another person's perspective, offering support without seeking personal gain and being genuinely interested in their wellbeing are markers of a true friend. These qualities attract similar souls, leading to mutually fulfilling relationships.

In a world increasingly dominated by digital interactions and superficial engagements, it is more important than ever to prioritise real-world connections. Social media may offer the illusion of connection but it often lacks the depth and sincerity of face-to-face interactions. Taking the time to meet someone in person, to share a moment without the filter of a screen, can bring immense joy and meaning.

Furthermore, diversity in your social circle can greatly enrich your perspective. Engaging with individuals from different backgrounds, cultures and walks of life broadens your understanding of the world. It challenges your assumptions, encourages growth and fosters empathy. These interactions, while sometimes uncomfortable, are deeply rewarding.

A rich social life is also about giving as much as receiving. Being there for others, offering your time, your ear or simply your presence can have a profound impact. Small acts of kindness often leave the biggest impressions. Whether it is helping someone move house, offering

encouragement during a tough time or just being a reliable presence, these efforts strengthen the fabric of friendship.

True richness is not something you can buy or inherit. It is built through moments that carry meaning and connection. The laughter shared on an ordinary evening, the comfort of an unspoken understanding, the quiet loyalty of someone who stays when things go wrong. These are the things that shape a life worth remembering.

If you wish to live a truly wealthy life, start with the people around you. Call someone. Invite them over. Go for a walk. Give them your attention. Make space for connection without an agenda. Let the bonds grow naturally. And as they grow, so will your own sense of purpose, of joy, of belonging.

Not everything needs to be grand. Often the smallest moments carry the most meaning. A conversation that lingers in memory, a kind gesture that was never forgotten, a shared silence that spoke volumes. These are the riches that no one can take from you.

Spend your time wisely. You may not carry anything with you at the end but what you leave behind in the hearts of others is more than enough.

Build Your Own Personal Library

Knowledge is the true currency for our mental well-being. No amount of money can purchase that kind of pleasure or satisfaction. If you think that consuming substances like magic mushrooms or smoking weed will bring you this lasting pleasure, then you are sorely mistaken. You should stop these harmful behaviours immediately. These substances are merely burning through your money to buy a fleeting blackout, a temporary escape that tricks your mind into a false sense of pleasure. It is never lasting. The moment you stop spending on these stimulants, the illusion fades, and you are left with nothing but a hollow craving. Eventually, you either exhaust your funds or face severe consequences, including risking your health or even your life.

On the other hand, reading has a remarkable ability to stimulate the mind in a positive, lasting way. It encourages critical thinking, a wonderful journey of stretching your mind to reach a deeper, more insightful state. After reading and thinking critically, a short meditation or quiet moment can help cool your brain down, much like a good sauna after an intense sports match. This calming phase allows the mind to process new ideas, rest, and prepare for the next challenge.

Many rich and successful business people, tech innovators, or even ordinary salaried workers share a common habit: they make reading a part of their daily routine. It is not because they want to cram every piece of knowledge in the world into their brains. That would be impossible. Instead, they use reading as a way to train their minds, much like how athletes train their bodies every day to maintain stamina and strength required for their sports or profession. Reading is a form of mental exercise designed to improve critical thinking skills so they can be ready for any question or problem that comes their way.

There is a widespread misconception that bosses do nothing in their offices besides shouting orders before going out for lunch, coffee, or

even golf. The reality is quite different. They spend a great deal of time processing problems and formulating strategies before giving out orders for execution. Their work relies heavily on their brains. The workers do the hands-on work, while the bosses use their mental strength and sharpness to guide the entire operation. That is why people respect their leaders and look up to them.

Many of these successful people keep a large personal library at home or in the office for exactly this purpose. They may read or simply enjoy the presence of books around them to create an atmosphere that constantly reminds their mind that knowledge is flowing in. You could start something like this in your own home by purchasing a cheap bookcase from a store like IKEA and filling it with books you enjoy. It does not need to be the latest bestseller or the most expensive edition from a fancy bookstore. It can simply be books that speak to your interests, ones you find at flea markets, second-hand bookstores, or even charity shops. The charm of these books lies not in their newness but in their relevance and the joy they bring you.

If you are more digitally inclined, you could invest in an eBook reader or tablet and store your entire library inside that device. However, I always recommend keeping physical books if possible. Our minds have been conditioned over time to associate physical books with knowledge, while tablet-like devices are often linked to entertainment. Just test yourself. How many times have you opened a book app only to get distracted by YouTube, Netflix, or other online distractions? In contrast, when you hold an actual book in your hands, you are more likely to focus and plan to finish at least a couple of chapters in one sitting.

If you cannot afford to build your own library or lack space at home, public libraries provide an excellent alternative. Many libraries today offer comfortable spaces with quiet corners to read, study, or simply relax. I discovered one nearby that even includes a decent café inside, allowing visitors to enjoy drinks as long as they do not spill them on the books. This combination turned the library into my regular hangout, a place where I could do my work, read whenever boredom crept in, and enjoy a good cup of coffee. I often spent hours there.

Before finding this library, I used to frequent places like Starbucks or other cafés to work or read. However, the library quickly became a second home. It offered bigger tables, fewer crowds, and far less noise. Moreover, the shelves held a wide range of relevant books that I could pull off anytime I needed to research something for work or personal interest. The convenience and atmosphere were unmatched compared to typical cafés, making it the perfect environment to cultivate knowledge. One of the greatest benefits of libraries is the access they offer to a vast pool of resources completely free of charge. Unlike buying every book you want to read, public libraries enable you to borrow books without any cost. You can explore genres and topics you would never normally consider because the financial risk is zero. This freedom encourages experimentation and broadens your horizons.

Libraries often provide access to digital learning platforms as well. Many have subscriptions to online courses, audiobooks, or magazines. By signing up with a library card, you can tap into these resources from the comfort of your home, effectively turning your device into a portable learning hub. These platforms cover everything from history and literature to coding and business skills, making lifelong learning accessible to everyone.

Beyond the physical and digital materials, libraries serve as community centres where like-minded individuals gather. They frequently organise workshops, book clubs, lectures, and discussion groups that promote interaction and deeper understanding. Joining such groups is a great way to meet new people who share your passion for learning and stimulate your intellectual growth through conversation.

Using libraries and free learning platforms is an investment in yourself. Unlike the temporary high from drugs or other destructive behaviours, the knowledge and skills you develop through reading and learning are assets that stay with you for life. They sharpen your mind, improve your decision-making, and increase your resilience in the face of challenges. This kind of growth is sustainable and enriching.

The habit of reading and learning can start small. Begin with topics that genuinely interest you. If you enjoy history, pick a historical biography or a book about an era that fascinates you. If fiction appeals more, find a novel in a genre you love. Gradually, as your mind expands, you will develop an appetite for more complex or diverse material. The key is consistency. Just as athletes train every day, a daily commitment to reading, even if only for a few minutes. It helps to build mental stamina over time.

Another important aspect is critical thinking. Reading alone does not suffice if you simply absorb information passively. To gain true benefit, you must engage actively with the material. Question what you read, challenge the assumptions presented, and weigh different viewpoints against one another. This mental exercise turns reading into a potent tool for personal growth and effective problem-solving. It encourages deeper understanding rather than superficial knowledge and builds the ability to navigate complexities with clarity. Without this active engagement, knowledge remains static; with it, learning becomes dynamic and transformative.

Once you have absorbed and analysed new information, allowing your mind to rest through meditation or quiet reflection consolidates your learning. It is like cooling down after a workout, preventing mental fatigue and preparing your brain for the next challenge.

In today's fast-paced world, it is tempting to seek quick fixes for pleasure or distraction. However, these shortcuts often come at a high cost. The real pleasure comes from growth, understanding, and the ability to navigate life's complexities with confidence and clarity. Knowledge is not just a means to an end; it is a source of joy in itself.

Limit Digital Noise

In today's hyperconnected world, social media is an omnipresent force shaping the way we think, feel, and live. It offers endless streams of information, entertainment, and connection, but it also brings with it a flood of noise. The constant barrage of posts, stories, and updates can clutter your mind and distort your perception of reality. If you want to live a life that feels meaningful and intentional, it is essential to learn how to limit digital noise and curate your digital space carefully.

One of the most damaging habits cultivated by social media is the tendency to compare yourself to others. When you scroll through endless feeds filled with polished images and success stories, it becomes easy to measure your worth by the lives of others. This comparison is not only futile but also harmful. You are unique, with your own path, challenges, and dreams. Chasing after the curated lives of strangers only drains your energy and steals your joy.

The first step to reducing this harmful comparison is to be deliberate about who you follow online. Seek out those who inspire a slow, thoughtful, and intentional lifestyle. These accounts focus on authenticity and encourage their followers to embrace simplicity and presence. They do not promote unrealistic perfection or materialistic values. Instead, they share content that fosters reflection, growth, and genuine connection.

There is absolutely no value in feeling jealous of others. When envy takes hold, it clouds your vision and blinds you to your own potential. Social media thrives on this vulnerability. Many posts are designed to trigger feelings of inadequacy or longing, encouraging users to chase after likes, views, and validation. This feeds the system that enriches so-called influencers and content creators at the expense of your mental wellbeing.

By giving in to jealousy, you are only helping to build their wealth and status. Sponsorships, advertisements, and brand deals come as a direct result of engagement metrics such as likes and views. The more you compare and envy, the more you feed their success and ego, both financially and psychologically. But there is nothing truly enviable about someone else's life when you consider the full picture. You do not see their struggles, failures, or moments of despair. Social media rarely reveals these aspects because they do not fit the narrative of success and happiness that attracts followers.

What truly matters is you and your journey. You hold the power to shape your own life, regardless of the constraints you face. It is perfectly natural to dream of enjoying luxuries or experiences that others showcase online. There is nothing wrong with wanting more comfort, joy, or freedom. Ambition is healthy, and it can be a powerful motivator. However, it is important to recognise your limitations, whether financial or otherwise, and work within them without resentment or frustration.

Almost everyone has constraints of some kind. Many influencers or content creators you admire did not get to where they are overnight. They invested tremendous amounts of effort, time, and sometimes personal sacrifice to reach their goals. What you see is often only the highlight reel of their achievements. Their setbacks, moments of doubt, and failures remain hidden, as they fear appearing weak or uninspiring. The public expects to see success stories and positivity, not the messy reality behind the scenes.

This selective portrayal can skew your understanding of success and make your own challenges seem greater by comparison. Recognising this can help you avoid falling into the trap of unrealistic expectations. Instead of competing with others, focus on enriching yourself. Use social media selectively and mindfully rather than allowing it to consume your attention and energy.

The ability to enjoy peace itself is a luxury. In a world where so many are caught in relentless noise and pressure, finding moments of calm and contentment is rare and precious. This peace comes not from external circumstances, but from within. It grows when you learn to detach from the chaos and distractions around you. Valuing this inner peace means protecting your mind from needless comparison, envy, and the endless scroll. It means understanding that true wealth is not measured by possessions or popularity, but by the quiet confidence that comes from knowing and accepting yourself.

A good practice is to transform social media from a source of distraction into a tool for inspiration. When you come across content that motivates you or sparks an idea, pause and reflect on how it can apply to your life. Then, set concrete goals inspired by those moments. Create small daily rituals or take up hobbies that nurture your interests and talents. By doing so, you reclaim your time and channel your energy into meaningful progress rather than endless scrolling.

Sharing your own experiences online can also be a positive practice if done with the right intention. Posting photos, videos, or stories does not have to be about showing off or seeking approval. Instead, it can serve as a personal record of your growth and achievements. Think of it as a digital journal or a time capsule that you and others can look back on to celebrate progress and shared joys.

For example, I once shared videos of my pets simply for fun. I did not worry about the number of likes, comments, or views. I posted them so my family and friends could enjoy these moments and also so I could revisit them in the future. These videos captured the playful antics, mischievous behaviour, and growth of my pets over time. To my surprise, some of the videos gained significant attention, attracting messages from pet product companies offering sponsorships.

However, I chose to decline those offers. While the idea of sponsorship might seem appealing, I did not want to be bound by contractual restrictions that could limit my creativity or force me to promote products that did not align with my values. My content was meant to be genuine and free, reflecting my personal enjoyment rather than commercial interests.

Although my channel did not grow into a large-scale influencer platform, I found satisfaction and contentment in this experience. I never intended to become a professional YouTuber, but the process taught me valuable lessons about how the business side of social media operates. It opened up possibilities for income streams I had never considered, and it expanded my understanding of digital marketing and audience engagement.

Yet, these were by-products rather than the primary goal. The real reward came from engaging in something I loved and sharing it with others on my own terms. This is a crucial lesson: authenticity and passion resonate more than manufactured content aimed solely at chasing metrics.

In contrast, many people get caught up in the pursuit of likes and views, allowing those numbers to dictate their self-worth and creative choices. This can lead to stress and even destructive behaviours. When you prioritise external validation over genuine expression, you risk losing your sense of identity and purpose.

To avoid this, cultivate patience and let your content evolve naturally. When your work is sincere, useful, or entertaining, it will find its audience. Whether it is sharing your daily challenges with a pet, demonstrating creative solutions, or documenting your hobbies, genuine content has intrinsic value. It may not go viral overnight, but it will gradually attract those who appreciate your authenticity.

It is also important to keep perspective about social media metrics. Likes, comments, and views are transient and often superficial indicators. They rarely capture the deeper impact your content may have on individuals who connect with it in meaningful ways. Instead of obsessing over numbers, focus on creating something that feels true to you.

Limiting digital noise goes beyond just social media. It involves a holistic approach to managing your digital environment. This means decluttering your devices, organising your apps and notifications, and setting boundaries on screen time. When you reduce distractions and the constant influx of alerts, you create space for clarity and presence.

Consider allocating specific times to check social media and messages instead of responding to every notification. This helps prevent mindless scrolling and promotes intentional consumption. Use digital tools and settings that block or filter distracting content, allowing you to focus on what truly matters.

In the end, your digital space should support your goals and wellbeing rather than detract from them. By curating who you follow, how you engage, and what you share, you reclaim control over your attention and your life.

Your journey is unique, and you have the power to direct it. Do not allow the noise of others' lives to drown out your own voice. Instead, invest in your dreams with patience and authenticity. Celebrate small victories and embrace the process of growth without rushing or comparing.

This way, you build a life rooted in intention and meaning rather than fleeting impressions. The digital world can be a powerful ally when approached mindfully, offering inspiration, connection, and opportunities. But it must be tamed and managed with care.

Remember, there is nothing to envy about the filtered, curated images of others. Your life, with all its imperfections and potential, holds the greatest value. Honour it by limiting noise, cultivating authenticity, and living genuinely. That is the true path to contentment and fulfilment.

Travel Thoughtfully

Luxury is not measured by price tags or passport stamps. It is found in perception, in the way we choose to experience what surrounds us. To travel thoughtfully is to live richly, even when our feet do not cross borders. When one begins to observe their own town with the curiosity usually reserved for foreign destinations, the streets start to change shape. Familiar pavements no longer appear dull. The chipped bricks of an old bakery begin to tell stories. Every corner reveals something that had been quietly waiting for attention.

It starts with a decision. Wake up on a Saturday and instead of reaching for your phone or rushing through breakfast, treat the morning like the beginning of a getaway. Choose your outfit carefully, not for anyone else but for yourself. A clean shirt, perhaps something with a collar, neatly ironed. A pair of shoes that feel firm beneath your soles. If you have a hat or scarf that makes you feel prepared for the day, wear it. Pack a small notebook or bring your phone for photographs. Today is not ordinary. It is an expedition, and your destination is just beyond your doorstep.

Begin by walking. Choose a direction you rarely take. Turn left where you usually turn right. Let the day stretch without plans. Stop in front of the windows. Peer into shop displays. Read the signs pinned to public notice boards. You might find a local chess club inviting players on Sunday afternoons or a poster advertising a jazz night in a community centre. These fragments of life often go unnoticed, yet they offer the richness of a culture quietly breathing beneath routine.

Wander into independent shops, even if you do not intend to buy anything. Step into that second-hand bookshop with the narrow entrance and uneven floorboards. Let your fingers trace the spines of books published fifty years ago. Read the dedications written on title pages. Sometimes a single sentence written by hand can offer more intimacy than an entire autobiography. Ask the shopkeeper how long they have been there. Let the conversation take shape without rushing. Listen. People open up when they feel they are being heard, and their stories become part of your journey.

Look up. Architecture tells the history of a place far better than any brochure. Notice the lines of the rooftops, the styles of window frames, the way one building leans slightly into the next. Each detail has a reason. Sometimes it is practical, sometimes purely aesthetic, but always meaningful. Follow the rhythm of a street until it takes you somewhere unexpected. A row of townhouses might lead to a narrow lane with a wrought iron gate. Push it open if it is public. Behind such gates there are often gardens, quiet courtyards, or forgotten spaces filled with overgrown ivy and worn benches. Sit for a while. Listen to the birds. Watch the leaves move. Stillness, when chosen deliberately, feels indulgent.

Do not underestimate the luxury of time. When you give yourself permission to experience a full afternoon without pressure or plans, you begin to notice what most people ignore. A woman walking her dog might hum a song you have not heard in years. A busker beneath an archway might play the violin with a sincerity that catches in your throat. These details are fleeting, but when you travel thoughtfully, you collect them like souvenirs.

Visit places that seem too ordinary to be destinations. Go to your local museum, even if it is just one room. Walk slowly through each display. Read every plaque. You might find a piece of history that connects directly to your street or surname. Often these spaces are maintained by volunteers, and a kind question can lead to stories never published. If there is a café nearby, sit and order something you do not usually choose. A tart, a pot of tea, something that feels like a treat. Eat slowly. Let the atmosphere around you become part of the flavour.

Churchyards, libraries, markets, and train stations all offer moments of richness if approached with awareness. A market stallholder may share where their honey is harvested or why they prefer one spice over another. A librarian might point you to a corner filled with local authors. The station might have a plaque honouring a historical figure who once passed through. These pieces, stitched together, form a narrative. And in that narrative you are no longer a local. You are a traveller.

If you live near the coast, walk its full length. Carry a sandwich wrapped in paper and find a dry patch of rock to sit and eat. If you are inland, find the river, the canal, the woodland path. Make space for silence. Let your thoughts wander without needing to solve anything. Write in your notebook if you are inclined. A paragraph describing the colour of the sky. A quote overheard in a shop. A sketch of an old house. These small acts record the journey.

Luxury is often mistaken for cost, but true luxury lies in depth. A thoughtfully experienced hour can offer more richness than a week spent rushing through airports and ticking off guidebook suggestions. It is not about where you are but how present you allow yourself to be. Choose to linger. Choose to notice. Choose to step inside the bakery you have passed a hundred times but never entered.

Attend local events. Watch a play performed by a community theatre group. Sit near the front, allow yourself to be drawn in. These performances are filled with energy and love, often with ticket prices low enough to be considered a gift. Visit school art exhibitions, seasonal fairs, poetry readings, or food festivals. Dress for the occasion, even if it is small. You do not need an invitation to feel part of something.

Speak to strangers when it feels natural. Compliment someone's coat or ask about the scent in a shop. Connection, no matter how brief, enhances travel. It creates warmth, and warmth is always a luxury. Keep your phone tucked away when possible. Let your senses take the lead.

Smell, sight, touch, and taste have a way of rooting us in the moment. When the senses are engaged, memory is formed with more strength.

Walk into parks. Not the manicured ones alone, but the overlooked spaces where trees grow a little wild. Watch children build towers with sticks. Notice how dogs greet one another with joy. Sit beside the old man feeding pigeons and ask him how long he has lived nearby. People carry maps of their own, and through them, the town becomes layered. What once seemed small reveals itself to be vast.

Travel thoughtfully by marking the passing of seasons. Visit the same places in winter and in spring. Watch how the light falls differently, how the sounds shift. A footpath covered in frost holds a different kind of beauty to the same one bathed in summer sunlight. Create rituals. A morning walk to a nearby hill every first Sunday. A monthly visit to a local café with a notebook. A yearly return to a particular spot where you once felt completely at ease.

Bring someone along now and then. Share the experience. Walk slowly with a friend, a partner, or a family member. Show them what you have discovered. Listen to what they notice. Their perspective will enrich your own. Take turns choosing the next destination. One day it might be an open garden event. Another day, a food stall under a railway arch. Experiences shared become stitched into memory with stronger thread.

Read about your town's history. The library, the council archives, even old online forums can offer glimpses into how places have changed. Find photographs from a hundred years ago and compare them to the streets as they are now. Walk the same paths. Look for remnants. An old fence post. A doorway. A name etched in stone. When you begin to see the layers of time, you begin to understand the depth of place.

Be mindful of how you spend, but do not be afraid to spend where it brings genuine value. A handmade candle from a small craft shop, a fresh loaf from a baker who rises before dawn, a ticket to a local lecture or recital. These are not indulgences. They are investments in culture, in community, in yourself. When you support what is near, you participate in its growth.

Photograph with purpose. Not for social media alone, but for your own documentation. Capture what speaks to you. A crooked lamp post. A mural fading with age. The way sunlight hits a particular brick wall at four in the afternoon. Collect these images and print a few. Keep them somewhere visible. Let them remind you of what is possible when you look closely.

Travelling thoughtfully teaches gratitude. It reveals how much beauty can be found without distance. It breaks the myth that escape is required for joy. When approached with care, a single street can offer as much wonder as a new country. The scent of bread, the colour of leaves, the sound of laughter through an open window. These are riches.

So step outside with a traveller's heart. Walk slowly. Speak kindly. Observe without judgement. Give yourself to the moment. Let each step uncover something new. That is how you live luxuriously with little money. That is how you travel without leaving home.

That is how you begin to live as though every day is an invitation to discover the world, even when the world is just around the corner.

Avoid Debt and Interest Traps

Avoiding the temptation of debt is one of the most critical aspects of achieving long-term financial stability and peace of mind. Many people fall into the debt trap because they confuse financial convenience with financial capacity. They borrow money not out of necessity, but to fund a lifestyle that appears impressive to others, even if it exceeds their current means. This behaviour, though increasingly normalised by advertising and social media, often leads to stress, anxiety, and in the worst cases, bankruptcy. True wealth lies not in showcasing material possessions, but in the mental calm that comes from being financially unburdened.

Borrowing to upgrade one's lifestyle may seem harmless at first. After all, why not enjoy a better phone, a bigger house, or a flashier car if it can be paid off in monthly instalments? However, this illusion of affordability is what traps many individuals into a cycle of debt. Interest payments, especially those that compound, quickly add up and inflate the actual cost of purchases. What initially seemed like a smart financial move often becomes an oppressive financial burden. This is especially true with credit cards, which are often marketed as tools for empowerment, but when used carelessly, become instruments of financial strain.

Credit cards can offer convenience and benefits, such as, airline miles, or purchase protection. However, they must be handled with strict discipline. They are not an extension of income. Treating them as extra cash leads to overspending and difficulty keeping track of actual financial limitations. The result is an accumulating balance that, if unpaid, begins to incur significant interest charges. These interest rates are often higher than those of other forms of credit, making credit card debt particularly dangerous.

Among young people globally, credit card debt has become a major factor leading to financial ruin. Many students and young professionals begin their adult lives with little financial education and are quickly enticed by the ease of using credit. What they do not always realise is that minimum payments barely reduce the principal balance, and interest compounds each month. Without a plan to pay the full balance monthly, what begins as a small, manageable debt can snowball into a significant liability. Once the balance grows beyond a certain point, it becomes harder to pay off, leading to stress, reduced credit scores, and in extreme cases, bankruptcy.

Financial prudence begins with understanding the nature of debt and being intentional about spending. A wise individual sees the credit card as a tool, not a crutch. They use it for daily necessities, carefully track spending, and pay the entire balance before the due date. This not only avoids interest but also builds a strong credit history. Rewards and perks should be secondary to maintaining a clear balance. Paying interest should never be part of the plan. The only way to truly benefit from the advantages of a credit card is to use it responsibly.

Banks are constantly in competition to attract more users to their credit cards. They offer sign-up bonuses, waive annual fees, and present flashy advertisements to appeal to a wide audience. In the current era where physical cash is becoming less common, digital transactions are rapidly taking over. E-wallets and loyalty apps now dominate the payment space, and they often incentivise linking credit cards to access membership perks or cashbacks. This convenience and gamified reward system make it even easier to lose track of spending. Financial discipline is more crucial than ever in this environment.

While linking credit cards to e-wallets or apps may seem like a smart way to earn points or discounts, it is essential to remember that these systems are designed to encourage more frequent spending. Every perk comes at the cost of forming spending habits that may not align with financial goals. Individuals must ask themselves whether the small benefits gained are worth the risk of accumulating unnecessary debt. If the balance cannot be paid off in full each month, then any benefit is cancelled out by the interest incurred.

The concept of lifestyle inflation is also tied closely to debt traps. As income increases, many feel the urge to upgrade their standard of living. While it is natural to want better things, the danger lies in letting expenses rise faster than income. Some justify purchases by assuming that future income will cover them, which is a risky mindset. It is far safer to upgrade slowly, only when finances comfortably allow for it without borrowing. This approach keeps financial goals intact and provides long-term satisfaction instead of short-term thrills.

Savings should always be prioritised over upgrades. A solid emergency fund, consistent investments, and low fixed expenses are the true markers of financial health. Borrowing should only occur for needs that have long-term value, such as education or home ownership, and even then, it must be approached with caution and a repayment strategy. Borrowing for wants, especially through high-interest credit, compromises future financial stability for momentary pleasure.

In an age where consumerism is encouraged and credit is easy to obtain, avoiding debt requires intentional effort. It means learning to say no to unnecessary expenses and delaying gratification. It means developing a budget and sticking to it, tracking expenses, and understanding where money is being spent. It also means understanding that financial freedom is not defined by how much one earns, but by how little one owes. Peace of mind comes from knowing that there are no looming payments or compounding interest waiting in the shadows.

Many people who have achieved financial freedom speak not of flashy cars or designer clothes, but of the joy that comes from not worrying about bills, from having the flexibility to change careers or travel without financial strain. This freedom is built on daily decisions that prioritise needs over wants, planning over impulse, and discipline over indulgence. Those who choose to live below their means, no matter their income level, consistently find themselves in stronger financial positions than those who chase status through borrowed money.

There is also an emotional and psychological cost to being in debt. It brings anxiety, affects relationships, reduces the ability to take risks, and creates a constant background stress that can erode overall well-being. Conversely, the absence of debt brings clarity, confidence, and a sense of control. It allows for better decision-making and opens up opportunities that would otherwise be blocked by financial obligations. Financial independence is not just about numbers; it is about quality of life.

Credit cards, if used wisely, can be beneficial tools. They can offer protection on purchases, serve as a buffer in emergencies, and make online transactions secure. However, the key lies in using them with full awareness of the consequences. No reward is worth the stress that comes from lingering debt. The goal should always be to stay in control, never to let convenience dictate financial choices. With every swipe, there should be a clear plan to repay, and a habit of treating borrowed money with the same seriousness as one's own savings.

The modern financial ecosystem is designed for speed, ease, and consumption. Apps allow one-click purchases, credit lines are pre-approved, and advertisements suggest that happiness lies in the next acquisition. But in this fast-paced, consumption-driven world, the wisest move is to slow down. To assess, to plan, and to resist the pressure to spend more than necessary. Living within one's means is not old-fashioned; it is timeless wisdom that guards against financial instability.

Those who learn early to value freedom over display, planning over impulse, and discipline over ease, will find themselves not only financially secure but mentally at peace. In the end, it is not about denying oneself joy, but about choosing the kind of joy that lasts, the kind that is not followed by stress or regret. Avoiding debt and interest traps is not just a financial strategy, it is a lifestyle philosophy that builds a foundation for a better, freer life.

Build A Strong Financial Foundation

To live a life of luxury, you need money. That is the simple truth. While this book may have offered ways to enjoy a luxurious lifestyle with minimal spending, if your vision of luxury includes expensive cars, a sprawling mansion, designer wardrobes, and long, indulgent holidays in exotic places, then you will need serious financial power to make it a reality.

This is the nature of the world we live in. Capitalism drives every major economy, whether it is declared openly or practised behind a mask. Even China, which labels itself a communist state, operates with unmistakable capitalist traits. Its people are driven by the same desire to accumulate wealth that shapes Western societies. That ambition to grow financially and acquire more stands in direct contradiction to their founding ideology. Still, the government allows it because it understands that suppressing individual economic growth would eventually spark unrest and erode their control. That is an entirely different discussion on its own, but it serves to show that wealth building is not only permitted but expected, regardless of political banners.

So if you want that luxurious lifestyle, where exactly do you get the money? One path is to work hard. Put in long hours, grind through your career, and chase promotions. You will eventually see your income grow. However, there is a cost. The higher the income, the more of your time is consumed by the job. You may earn a large salary, but you find yourself too exhausted to enjoy any of it. You come home late, weekends vanish into recovery, and your social life becomes a memory. You have money, but no freedom. I know this from personal experience. I had the earnings, but there was no time left to spend them.

To skip that slow climb and achieve your goals faster, many turn to loans. You walk into a bank, sign a contract, and walk out with the money needed to buy your dream car, your house, or a once-in-a-lifetime vacation. At first, it feels like freedom. But when the month ends, you see the numbers. A huge portion of your salary is swallowed up by monthly instalments, interest charges, and credit card bills. The leftovers are barely enough to get by.

You are surrounded by symbols of success, yet feel suffocated by the burden they carry. You got the luxury, but in exchange, you gave up the comfort of living freely. Now you sit inside your new car or in the living room of your beautiful home, staring at your bank app and wondering if this really counts as a luxurious life. It may look glamorous from the outside, but deep down, it feels more like you are wearing the mask of a millionaire while living like a servant to your own expenses.

To live the life you truly desire, it becomes essential to build multiple streams of income that work together to multiply your money. Picture this concept as having a basket filled with various fruits. You eat the fruit, gaining nourishment and satisfaction from its sweetness and vitality. Most people see the seeds inside as useless, something to be discarded without a second thought, tossed casually into the garbage bin.

Yet, if you take those seemingly worthless seeds and plant them carefully, over time they might grow into trees. These trees will eventually bear fruit, providing you with an endless supply. You can then consume the fruit and plant the seeds once again. By repeating this process, what began as a simple basket of fruit could transform into a vast orchard.

This analogy fits perfectly with the idea of investing your extra cash. When you start, the amount may appear small and insignificant. It feels like a drop in the ocean, hardly enough to make a difference. However, if you leave that money to grow by reinvesting the dividends you earn from those investments, it has the potential to multiply steadily. The dividends act like the seeds, small returns that might seem insignificant at first, but when planted back into the investment, they contribute to the growth of your portfolio. Over several years of careful investing, avoiding reckless losses, and following a strategy that fits your risk tolerance and goals, those dividends will become more substantial. At some point, they could grow large enough to buy you something practical or enjoyable, such as a new phone.

Once you have identified an investment strategy that consistently works for you, repeating it becomes key. The dividends you earn will increase in size and frequency, allowing you to cover bigger expenses over time. You might find yourself using the dividends to pay for your dream vacations, the car you have always wanted, or even a house that you have dreamed of owning. It is important to recognise that in the beginning, the money generated may only cover the monthly instalments on these purchases rather than the full cost. Nonetheless, having the dividends contribute to these payments grants you a form of financial freedom. It lets you use your salary with greater flexibility because a portion of your expenses is already taken care of by your investment income.

At this stage, however, you may find that the dividends are not merely for spending. Since you have found a strategy that works and provides reliable returns, you could choose to reinvest a significant portion of those dividends. By doing so, you continue to grow your portfolio at an accelerated rate. The cycle of investing, earning dividends, and reinvesting those dividends fuels an upward spiral of wealth creation. What once was a small seed planted in a basket now becomes a thriving orchard that produces fruit year after year.

This process of creating multiple income streams requires patience and discipline. It is not about quick wins or sudden large gains but about steady, consistent growth over time. Like tending to an orchard, it needs attention, care and the right conditions to flourish. The initial stages may feel slow or even discouraging, but the rewards of persistence become evident as your portfolio and dividends grow steadily. By continuing to nurture your investments and reinvesting the returns, you set yourself on a path where money works for you instead of the other way around.

This strategy does not simply increase your wealth; it reshapes your relationship with money. Instead of relying solely on your active income, the income generated from your investments provides an additional layer of financial security. It may start with something as modest as paying for a phone, but it expands to cover larger goals and even the cost of monthly obligations. Over time, those obligations become easier to handle, leaving you with more freedom to pursue your passions, hobbies and dreams without the constant worry of how to pay the bills.

Each cycle of investing and reinvesting brings you closer to the life you envision. It turns what might have been a small amount of money, easily overlooked or spent without thought, into a powerful tool for long-term financial independence. Just as a single seed grows into a tree and a tree into an orchard, your financial efforts compound and multiply, offering returns far beyond your initial investment. The key is to start early, be consistent and maintain the discipline to keep reinvesting your earnings.

Freedom is a rare luxury in life. Financial freedom, even more so, because nearly everyone remains bound to the need to make a living, not just now but throughout history and into the future. There is a sharp contrast between adults and children. Children move through their days without burdens or anxieties. Their laughter fills the air as they run, play, and explore the world with carefree joy. Meanwhile, many adults find themselves shackled by debts, obligations, and the relentless pressure to secure enough money, not just for themselves, but for those they care about. The weight of these responsibilities can feel like chains wrapped tightly around their very existence, leaving little room for peace or spontaneity. It is no wonder then that people glance at those young faces and feel a pang of envy, wishing they could return to a time when worries were few and smiles were effortless.

I will not be listing out specific tips or methods on how to build your financial portfolio within these pages, as that is not the purpose of this book. Instead, what I want to emphasise is the importance of conducting your own thorough research before making any investment decisions. The financial world can be complex and confusing, and blindly following advice or investing in something simply because it seems popular or familiar can be a costly mistake. Many people fall into the trap of purchasing stocks in companies they admire or brands they like without fully understanding the risks involved or the true state of the business. For example, you might be attracted to a brand because you enjoy their products or trust their reputation, and feel eager to become a shareholder. However, investing with that mindset can lead to disappointment. It is crucial to look beyond the surface and take the time to examine the company's financial health closely.

Start by gathering information about its cash flow, profit margins, and overall stability. Look into how consistent its dividend payments have been over time and whether it has a clear and realistic future plan for growth. Equally important is understanding the leadership behind the company. The background, experience, and integrity of top management can have a significant impact on how well the company performs in the long term. To help with this evaluation, create a checklist that includes all these factors so you can assess every potential investment against the same criteria. If all aspects meet your standards and no red flags arise, then it may be a suitable choice for your portfolio.

Avoid letting emotions influence your investment decisions. Investing based on personal feelings or loyalty to a brand is no different from gambling in a casino, where the odds are usually against you and the chance of loss is high. Instead, focus on the facts and figures, analysing data and trends with a clear head. The discipline of investing requires patience, careful thought, and a rational approach to risk.

Be cautious of the many paid courses or seminars offered by self-proclaimed investment experts online. These so-called "gurus" often promise quick profits or secret strategies, but their advice can be misleading or overly simplistic. It is better to rely on the vast amount of credible information that is freely available. Take advantage of resources such as TED Talks, educational videos, and presentations by experienced investors who share their knowledge without cost. By doing so, you can learn at your own pace, develop a deeper understanding of investment principles, and build a solid foundation for making informed decisions.

The path to financial success begins with education and careful preparation. Always question what you hear and verify it with your own research. In the end, investing wisely means empowering yourself with knowledge rather than hoping for luck.

Knowledge will make you money. Ignorance will only allow others to make money from you.

Be Generous to Others

Always practise generosity towards others. Give your time, your presence, your support, and your encouragement freely. These may seem like small gestures, but they carry immense value.

Generosity does not always have to come in the form of money or material possessions. Sometimes, the most meaningful gift you can offer someone is simply being there when they need you. Listening without judgement, offering words of reassurance, or showing up when others stay silent can leave a lasting impact.

When you choose to be generous, you begin to build a different kind of wealth. It is not the type measured in currency or possessions, but in the strength of your relationships and the depth of your connections. It adds meaning to your life, creates trust, and fosters a sense of belonging. In the long run, these are the things that truly sustain you, far beyond what money ever could.

That kind of experience is not something money can buy. But it gives you a sense of control, a feeling that you have the power to make a real difference in someone's life. Just by being generous with your time or support, you could change something important for someone. And the best part is, it feels good. It feels like a luxury, but without spending anything. Helping others like that gives you a kind of satisfaction that money alone could never match.

There was a time when I was travelling in a country in Asia. I was wandering through a crowded street filled with stalls selling all kinds of local food and snacks when something caught my eye from across the road. It was an old granny with a noticeable hunchback, slowly collecting cardboard boxes from a nearby shop. She was having a hard time folding them properly. Her hands trembled with age, but she kept pushing through, determined to finish. It was clear this was her only way to earn a living.

Just as I was about to approach and offer my help, a couple, tourists from China, stepped in before I could. The woman bought her some food and a drink. This small act of kindness seemed to brighten the granny's face. Meanwhile, the man got to work folding the cardboard boxes quickly and carefully stacking them into her trolley, which had a broken wheel that made it wobble dangerously. He asked where she was headed with the boxes, but she declined to let him help any further. Instead, she bowed repeatedly to them. The kind of deep, sincere bow showed her heartfelt gratitude.

After the couple left, she started stacking the rest of her collected bottles onto the trolley. She tried to push it along, but the broken wheel made the trolley jerk and catch on the uneven pavement. Seeing this, I stepped over and offered to help push it to the recycling centre. The centre was just a short walk away. She hesitated at first, politely refusing, but I insisted. What took me only ten minutes would probably have taken her at least three times as long.

When we reached the recycling point, the staff began weighing the bottles and cardboard to determine her payment. While they were busy, I quietly slipped some cash into her hand. At first, she looked shocked and pushed the money away. She said she could not accept anything after I had already helped her. I told her to please take it, explaining it was not much, maybe thirty or forty US dollars, but it would be enough to help her get through the next few days, maybe even a week if she was careful with it. After a moment, she finally accepted the money. Tears began to well in her eyes and traced slow paths down her deeply wrinkled cheeks.

It struck me then how someone her age should be enjoying retirement and not struggling out on the streets gathering recyclables. Quietly, she shared a heartbreaking story. Her son had been paralysed from the waist down in an accident a few years earlier. The driver responsible had fled the scene and they did not have enough money to hire a lawyer to seek justice. Her son was unable to provide enough information to the police to track the driver down. The weight of their hardship was clear in her voice.

I wanted to give her more money to somehow ease their burden, but she gently refused. She said something that stuck with me, something many of us might feel ashamed to admit when we hear it,

"I am still able to move, so I should earn the living myself, no matter how hard it is. It is not the responsibility of others to help me just because of my situation."

After that, I said goodbye to her and walked away, not realising when my eyes began to fill with tears. My life was far from perfect. I was not born with a silver spoon in my mouth. Yet my parents had managed to provide a decent life for us, one where we never had to worry about having enough to eat.

I could have spent the money on a nice bag from one of the shops along the street. I could have used it to buy a proper meal at a restaurant. But none of that would have brought me the same satisfaction as knowing my money had actually helped someone. It eased her burden, brought a smile to her face, and filled the stomachs of both her and her son. That feeling is far better than the brief happiness that comes from buying a designer bag, which lasts only a week before your eyes move on to the next one. This feeling and experience stayed with me for much longer, almost like it would last forever.

Many wealthy people turn to charity and become philanthropists because luxury goods lose their appeal over time. When designer bags, expensive cars, and lavish lifestyles become everyday normal, they no longer provide the thrill or sense of fulfilment they once did. Material possessions can only satisfy so much before they start to feel empty.

For some rich individuals, there is a deeper need to find meaning and purpose beyond accumulating wealth. Giving back through philanthropy offers a way to fill that void. It allows them to make a positive impact on others' lives, create lasting change, and find a sense of connection and contribution that money alone cannot buy. In that way, generosity becomes a source of true satisfaction that no amount of luxury can replace.

When you give without expecting anything in return, you open yourself to unexpected blessings. Life has a way of circling kindness back, often when you need it the most and from the places you least anticipate. True generosity carries no conditions. It comes from a sincere place, a quiet desire to help or share, not from calculation or the hope of reward.

If your actions are driven by the desire to gain, then the energy you send out is not of compassion but of transaction. The universe recognises that. Giving with strings attached is not giving at all. It becomes a masked form of self-interest, and in time, such intentions reveal themselves through disappointment or emptiness when the expected returns do not arrive.

Genuine giving carries a different weight. It brings peace, fulfilment, and a sense of meaning that lingers long after the act itself. The reward may not always come in the form of money or material gains. Sometimes, it returns as goodwill from others, unexpected opportunities, or moments of clarity and joy that shift the course of your life for the better.

Hoarding up creates a blockage, giving away creates the void for good things to come.

Prioritise Experiences Over Possessions

In today's society, the pressure to accumulate possessions can feel overwhelming. Advertisements and social media relentlessly promote the idea that owning the latest gadget, wearing the trendiest clothing or living in the biggest house will lead to happiness. Yet, time and again, both research and personal experience reveal that material things provide only fleeting satisfaction. True richness in life stems from the experiences we collect, not the items we accumulate.

Choosing to invest your time and energy in meaningful experiences is a wise decision, particularly when finances are tight. Experiences add texture, variety and depth to your life in ways that possessions simply cannot match. They create lasting memories and open opportunities to connect with others on a deeper level. Unlike products that may lose their shine, become outdated or break, the value of an experience can grow stronger over time, becoming a treasured part of your story.

Nature walks provide an excellent example of an experience that costs very little but offers enormous benefits. Stepping outside to explore nearby parks, woodlands or coastal trails allows you to slow down and truly appreciate the world around you. Feeling the fresh air on your skin, hearing the gentle rustle of leaves or birdsong, and witnessing the subtle changes of the seasons all work to reduce stress and lift your spirits. Taking time for yourself in this way reconnects you with the present moment and reminds you of life's simple but profound pleasures.

Volunteering at cultural events or community projects opens doors to new experiences and connections. Offering your time to causes that matter to you creates a sense of purpose and belonging. These opportunities often bring you into contact with people from diverse backgrounds, broadening your understanding of different perspectives.

Along the way, you may discover hidden talents or develop new passions. The joy derived from contributing to something larger than yourself often brings satisfaction far deeper than any monetary reward.

Exploring free exhibitions, public lectures or workshops is another way to enrich your life without spending much money. Museums and galleries frequently host events that educate and inspire, while libraries organise talks and courses covering a wide range of topics. Taking advantage of these resources nurtures your mind and fuels your curiosity. You gain new knowledge, meet people with similar interests and spark your creativity without the need to spend a fortune.

Hosting dinners at home is one of the most rewarding experiences you can offer yourself and your loved ones. Inviting friends and family to share a meal you have prepared creates warmth and intimacy that no restaurant can replicate. Cooking together or simply enjoying good food and conversation strengthens bonds and fosters a sense of community. These gatherings become special occasions where stories are shared, laughter rings out and memories are formed. They serve as a powerful reminder that richness often arises from the connections we nurture rather than the money we spend.

Prioritising experiences also encourages a more mindful way of living. When your focus shifts from acquiring possessions to engaging fully with what you do, you learn to be present in each moment. Experiences demand your attention and invite you to observe, feel and participate deeply. This awareness enhances your enjoyment and leaves a lasting impression on your heart and mind. It becomes easier to resist the pull of constant consumption and instead appreciate the here and now.

Experiences frequently challenge you to grow as a person. Travelling to new places, trying unfamiliar activities or meeting people from different walks of life broadens your horizons and builds resilience. These moments cultivate empathy, adaptability and confidence. They expand your understanding of the world and your role within it. Such personal development cannot be purchased or measured by material possessions.

It is important to recognise that experiences need not be extravagant or costly. They might be as simple as a walk to watch the sunset, a picnic in a local park, a visit to a neighbour's garden or a quiet evening spent reading a book. Small moments, enjoyed with intention and attention, often hold the greatest value. True richness lies in the quality and meaning of the experience rather than the price attached to it.

Choosing experiences over possessions also helps break free from the relentless cycle of wanting more. The craving for the newest item can quickly become exhausting and ultimately unsatisfying. Each purchase may bring a brief thrill only to be replaced by the desire for the next thing. Experiences, on the other hand, build a sense of fulfilment that deepens with time. They create stories worth telling, lessons to carry forward and feelings that endure. By investing in moments rather than things, you uncover a deeper and more lasting form of wealth.

Experiences foster generosity and connection. Sharing adventures, learning alongside others or simply spending time in good company strengthens relationships. These shared moments become part of your collective history and weave closer bonds. The joy found in giving your time, attention and care to others often exceeds any pleasure derived from material gifts.

Change your mindset

We have always been taught that earning more money is the key to living a better life. From a young age, we are made to believe that financial success is the ultimate measure of security and happiness. While it is undeniably true that money plays a crucial role in our survival, especially in a world that places such heavy value on material wealth, and while it certainly brings a sense of comfort, stability, and even confidence, the constant chase for more can quietly take something away from us. In the process of running after pay rises, promotions, and bigger numbers in the bank account, we often find ourselves feeling poorer in other parts of life. We lose time, peace of mind, meaningful relationships, and sometimes even our sense of purpose. The more we chase it, the more it slips into the centre of everything, and before we know it, we are measuring life by how much we earn rather than how much we truly live.

We tend to lose out on so much when our only goal in life is to make more money. Sure, you might be driving that luxury car, living in a grand mansion, indulging in fine dining, and buying designer products whenever you feel like it. From the outside, it might appear that you have everything you could ever want. But are those things truly more valuable than having a genuine friend who listens to you, or spending uninterrupted, meaningful time with your loved ones? You could be pulling in a six-figure salary, yet always tied up at work, constantly missing out on the little milestones that matter the most. The first time your child walks. Their school performances. Their graduation day. The proud moment they win their first medal at a sports meet. These are the moments that do not come back. And while you may believe that you are doing the right thing, working tirelessly to earn enough to send them to a top university so that they can secure a bright future, what you are truly sacrificing is the bond that connects you to them. They grow up viewing you not as a parent who stood by them, but as a provider, an ATM machine they only turn to when they need something. I have witnessed this play out far too often. Friends and clients have confided in me, expressing their sadness and confusion over the emotional distance between them and their children. Despite all their hard work and success, they do not feel close to their own families. One friend, in particular, admitted how distant he had become from his kids after years of working abroad, chasing a high-paying job that kept him away from home for most of their childhood. He missed it all. The laughter, the tantrums, the bonding. And now, he is just a stranger in their lives.

I am not saying that money is a bad thing, nor am I suggesting that one should stop striving to earn a little extra in order to provide a better life for their family. That would be unrealistic. What I am saying is that there needs to be a balance. One should not be so focused on accumulating wealth that they forget to invest in what truly brings lasting fulfilment: the richness of life itself and the relationships that come with it. The experiences you share with your loved ones, the memories you create together, those are the real treasures that stay with you. In many ways, they are like the currency of the heart and mind, filling you up in a way that money never could. You will always feel wealthier when you have a close, loving relationship with your family, than someone who might be financially successful but constantly surrounded by conflict and unhappiness at home. I have come across many people who have everything money can buy, yet suffer under the weight of fractured relationships, cold silence at the dinner table, and unresolved tensions that money simply cannot fix. In contrast, having peace, love, and warmth in your home makes you feel like the richest person in the world.

Have you ever wondered why it often feels like the more you desperately want something, the harder it becomes to get? It is a strange phenomenon that many people have experienced at some point. Things rarely seem to go smoothly when you are too fixated on them. Take the example of craving the latest iPhone. Even though your current phone is still perfectly functional, you find yourself longing for the new model.

That desire grows, but along with it comes a flood of anxiety. You start worrying about your upcoming bill payments, your rent, and all the other financial obligations you have. The craving creates pressure. And even if you do end up buying it, the joy is short-lived. That same pressure returns, perhaps even worse this time, as you now have to figure out how to pay off the next credit card bill or manage your expenses for the month.

There was a Guru I met during my journey to understand mindfulness and explore meditation techniques. One of the things he said left a deep impression on me. He explained,

"If you crave for something, you are creating a blockage, a disruption in your energy as you are too focused on that one goal, abandoning others."

That single statement stuck with me. Instead of forcing things to happen, he advised,

"State your goal and let it flow."

From my interaction with the Guru, I realised that it was essential to shift the mentality from "more is better" to "less is more." You might have heard about the 80-20 rule, which suggests that you put in 20% of the effort to get 80% of the return. This concept resonated deeply with me because it emphasised focusing on what truly matters instead of chasing every single desire or distraction.

When you apply this principle to life, it means identifying the few key things that bring the greatest value and satisfaction, rather than trying to do everything or accumulate more possessions. For example, rather than working long hours trying to earn extra money for things you do not really need, you concentrate on building meaningful relationships, honing a few important skills, or enjoying quality time with your family.

The Guru also taught me that constantly craving more only scattered my energy and attention, leaving me feeling drained and unfulfilled. By simplifying my goals and focusing on the essentials, I was able to find more clarity and peace. Instead of trying to force success or happiness, I learned to allow things to unfold naturally, trusting that what was meant for me would come in its own time.

This shift did not happen overnight, but gradually I began to notice a change. I felt less stressed about acquiring things or reaching for endless goals. My mind became quieter, and I could appreciate what I already had. The craving that once pulled me in many directions settled into a calm sense of contentment.

This lesson has stayed with me, reminding me that sometimes, having less focus and fewer desires leads to a richer, more balanced life. It encouraged me to practise mindfulness not only in meditation but also in daily living, by being present and grateful for the moment rather than always chasing what is next.

Show Gratitude in Everything You Have Now

You will not feel rich until you learn to stop measuring your life by what is missing. That lesson will not come easily, because everything around you trains you to do the opposite. From the moment you open your eyes in the morning, you are surrounded by messages that tell you you are not enough, that you have not arrived. You are told, again and again, that you are behind. That you need more. That if you do not have the house, the car, the investments, the side hustle, the curated holidays and the polished online profile, then you are failing. This pressure is relentless. It invades your thoughts and colours your self-worth. That pressure does not ease when your income grows. In many cases, it sharpens. With every raise, every new acquisition, you climb another rung on the ladder, but the ladder does not end. You find yourself in a cage built from comparisons, one rung higher than before, but a cage all the same. You are trapped by your own expectations, by society's standards, by the constant demand to do more, have more, be more.

Gratitude is not the feel-good answer to that pressure. It is the hard answer. It is the correction your mind needs, the clarity your soul requires. Gratitude is the ability to see clearly what is still intact, what is still beautiful, what is still worthy of recognition, even when your surroundings do not change and when your circumstances feel stuck or difficult. It is a discipline, a way of looking at life that resists the endless hunger for more. Gratitude asks you to notice the good that already exists, even when it is small or quiet. It demands honesty. It does not pretend problems do not exist. It does not deny hardship. It simply allows you to hold your difficulties and your blessings at once, without being overwhelmed by either.

I am not speaking about writing in a notebook once a day and pretending your problems are gifts. I am not talking about hollow optimism or the kind of forced positivity that dismisses pain and struggle. I am talking about a real, inner shift. A change that stops your peace from being held hostage by external milestones, by achievements and material signs of success. This shift means learning to find a calm place inside yourself that no money, no status, no external approval can take away. It means understanding that peace and contentment come from a deep acceptance of what is, rather than the relentless pursuit of what could be.

If you want to live richly with little, you have to build the skill of noticing what is already working. This does not mean ignoring your challenges or pretending they do not exist. It means anchoring yourself in what is real and solid in your life, no matter how small it seems. There is no richness possible in a mind that constantly obsesses over what it has not yet earned. There is no freedom in thinking that everything valuable sits just outside your reach, shimmering like a prize you must chase endlessly. True richness begins when you stop chasing and start seeing. It begins when you learn to live in the present moment with clear eyes and an open heart.

I have seen people with six-figure salaries panic when the stock market drops by two percent. I have watched them refresh their portfolio apps compulsively, forgetting to enjoy the house they already live in, the health they still have, the meals they share with their children. These are not greedy people. Many of them are generous, thoughtful, and deeply tired. But they have trained their minds to register only growth. Anything else feels like failure, even if it is just a moment of calm or stability. For them, gratitude is like learning to speak a language they never studied. A language that honours what is sufficient, rather than what is scarce.

And then there are people with very little, people with tight incomes, worn-out jobs, basic housing, who carry themselves with a kind of calm that cannot be faked. They pay attention to the rain on the window. They notice when their fridge is full. They observe when the pain in their joints eases. They feel when the night is quiet and no one in their family is sick. These are not saintly people. They are not putting on a show or performing for anyone. They simply see their lives without distortion. That clarity, that refusal to take what they have for granted, is what lets them feel something close to peace. It is a peace born from recognition and acceptance, not from denial.

If you have ever had a stretch of life where everything was in motion, illness, debt, loss, then you know how quickly the basics become precious. When you come out the other side, if you are lucky, you remember. You remember what it felt like to have a solid roof over your head. A warm drink in your hands. A body that still functions well enough to carry you through the day. Someone picking up your call when you need them most. Someone offering help without making you feel small or ashamed. These simple things become anchors when everything else feels fragile or uncertain.

That memory is what keeps you grounded. That is gratitude without illusion. It is not performative. It does not need an audience. It is the quiet habit of registering sufficiency. It is the gentle acknowledgement that, in this moment, what you have is enough to stand on. This form of gratitude is a steady foundation beneath the storm of life's challenges.

There were times when I ignored this entirely. When I made more money than I ever thought I would. When I bought things that I thought might impress someone, or buy me relief, or distract me from exhaustion. And there were moments where it worked, briefly. But the tiredness always returned. The bitterness lingered beneath the surface. The noise in my head told me nothing I did was enough. I looked successful to the outside world. But inside, I was numb. In that numbness, I missed what had once meant something to me, the simple moments, the small joys, the quiet certainties.

The act of returning to gratitude was not romantic. It was sobering. It was me sitting alone in a quiet room with no music and no screens, just looking around and asking myself what was still good. What was still solid. I found I could breathe again. I had someone to speak to. I had a meal. My body had not given up on me. That was where I started from. That was where I returned to time and again.

You can live richly with little only if you stop waiting for abundance to appear like a prize you have to win. The richness is already in your view. It might not be dramatic. It might not come with fireworks or grand announcements. But it is real. It is there. And it is enough to begin from. The trick lies in changing the lens through which you see your life. So many chase after the grander picture, always reaching forward, eyes on what is missing, constantly dissatisfied. They think richness is about arriving somewhere else, owning something they do not yet have, or being someone entirely different. But that mindset makes you blind to what is already within reach.

Richness is not just wealth in the financial sense. It is a measure of meaning, of stability, of peace. It is the way a quiet morning feels when you wake without anxiety. It is a warm cup of tea with someone who listens, a chair you love sitting in, a skill you have taken time to learn well. These are the things that build a life of quiet richness.

Build your life around what is already strong. Reinforce what you do have. Honour it. Use it wisely. That is gratitude in action. That is how you grow something sustainable, something that will not vanish when the next crisis comes or when your circumstances shift. Something that remains steady beneath the waves.

Take a look at what holds steady when all else feels uncertain. Is it your discipline? Your patience? Your ability to start over without bitterness? Those are the foundations. Strength does not always roar. Sometimes, it whispers. You must recognise it. Water it. Let it deepen its roots.

You do not need to chase more if what you already have is enough to carry you with dignity, with clarity, and with quiet purpose. When you recognise your resources and give them your attention, they multiply, not always in quantity, but in depth, in value, and in meaning.

Not everything has to be more. Sometimes, something lasting and quietly resilient is better. It is better for your peace. Better for your soul. Better for the life you want to live.

Seek growth, not just gain. Let your life be built with care, not haste. What endures is what matters. The rest is noise.

Luxury is not a measure of wealth or possession but a condition of the soul. The world teaches us to equate luxury with the accumulation of things such as gold, jewels, grand houses, and exotic pleasures. Yet, if we look beneath this surface, we discover that such riches are merely shadows cast by an insatiable desire for more. True luxury is not in acquiring but in knowing, not in having but in being.

Consider time. It is the most precious luxury, yet it cannot be bought or sold. It flows ceaselessly, indifferent to our wealth or status. To possess time, to hold it gently and choose how to spend it, is a luxury beyond the grasp of kings or paupers. When one pauses to reflect on this, money seems a poor substitute for the richness of a single unhurried moment, a deep breath, or a quiet mind.

Luxury arises from freedom, the freedom to exist without the chains of want or fear. It is the silence between the noise, the space between thoughts, the clarity that emerges when we shed the unnecessary. To live luxuriously is to be liberated from the tyranny of external validation and to find contentment in the essence of life itself.

In this sense, luxury becomes a paradox because it demands less, not more. It calls us to empty our hands and open our hearts to appreciate the invisible gifts that surround us: the softness of a breeze, the weight of a loved one's presence, the light that shifts across a room. These are luxuries that cannot be commodified.

So, when we seek luxury in money, we chase a mirage. The true luxury is the quiet knowing that enough is enough, that the self is whole, and that the present moment is complete. To understand this is to glimpse the profound difference between possession and presence, between being wealthy and being rich. It is here, in this recognition, that luxury reveals itself as the purest form of freedom.

In The End

This book has explored many ways to live a rich and luxurious life without relying on excessive spending. From renting instead of buying, embracing minimalism that is pleasing to the eye, choosing quality over brand names, and becoming your own chef, these are conscious decisions that improve your life without draining your bank account. These choices are not temporary hacks; they build a sustainable and deeply satisfying lifestyle.

Living richly begins with caring for yourself in every way. Prioritising your health means investing in the future of your body and mind. It is far less costly to maintain good health with proper nutrition, regular exercise, and enough rest than to face the expenses and discomfort of illness later on. When you have energy and vitality, your confidence grows naturally and you can engage fully with life. Sophistication is not about expensive clothes or flashy possessions, it is how you carry yourself, how you communicate, and the respect you show to others and yourself. Developing this kind of grace leaves a lasting impression and creates opportunities that no amount of money can buy.

Investing in personal development is one of the most valuable things you can do. Learning new skills, expanding your knowledge, and improving your emotional intelligence open doors that money alone cannot unlock. Public speaking, time management, and conflict resolution are examples of skills that enhance both your career and personal life. Cultivating a rich social life is just as important. Genuine friendships and meaningful connections provide support, joy, and growth. These relationships are treasures that outlast any material possession.

In today's world, limiting digital noise is crucial. The constant bombardment of information and distractions pulls your attention away from what matters most. By consciously reducing screen time and focusing on real-world experiences, you cultivate mindfulness and presence. Thoughtful travel enriches your perspective. It is not the number or cost of trips that matters but the quality of the experiences and lessons you take away. Avoiding debt and the interest trap is essential for true freedom. Living within your means, paying off what you owe, and steering clear of unnecessary loans give you control over your life and peace of mind.

Generosity is another pillar of living richly. Giving your time, knowledge, or resources to others builds goodwill and strengthens community. This generosity does not require wealth; simple acts of kindness make a difference and create a sense of abundance. Yet none of these principles can fully take hold without a fundamental change in mindset. The biggest obstacle is the belief that more money means a better life. This false idea causes many to chase possessions and status endlessly, often at the cost of their well-being and relationships.

Shifting your mindset from “more is better” to “less is more” changes everything. It allows you to appreciate simplicity, find joy in small things, and pursue goals that align with your values. When success is measured not by possessions but by peace, satisfaction, and connections, you unlock a far richer existence.

Living richly with little money requires discipline, intention, and courage. It means saying no to excess and distractions and yes to what builds your character and fulfils your heart. It means choosing quality over quantity, investing in yourself, nurturing your relationships, and living with clear purpose. It calls for constant commitment to growth, reflection, and kindness.

Remember, richness is not in your bank balance but in your experience of life. It is the peace you feel when your needs are met, the excitement of learning something new, the comfort of being with loved ones, and the satisfaction of living authentically. These are the true luxuries that bring lasting happiness.

As you continue your journey, keep making choices that add real value to your life. Keep developing your skills, deepening your relationships, and simplifying your surroundings. Embrace mindfulness and generosity. Know that the richest life is within your reach and does not depend on wealth but on your mindset and actions.

You have the power to live richly, no matter your income or status. Choose to live intentionally, wisely, and generously. That is the greatest luxury of all.